S0-AKO-316

JUMP
AND THE NET WILL APPEAR

How I Discovered the Art
of Personal Achievement and
the Rhythm of Success

ROBIN
CROW

Legacy Communications Group
Franklin, TN 37064

Jump . . . and the Net Will Appear   Copyright 1999, Robin Crow

All rights reserved. No part of this publication may be reproduced, stored in a retrieval system, or transmitted in any form or by any means—electronic, mechanical, photocopy, recording, or any other—except for brief quotations in printed reviews, without the prior permission of the publisher.

Jacket photography by Ron Keith / Cover design by Scott Bonner
Cover layout by Richmond & Williams / Typography by Becky Earls

Request for bulk sales, discounts, editorial permissions, or other information should be addressed to the publisher: Legacy Communications Group, Inc. 251 Second Avenue South, Franklin, Tennessee 37064

ISBN 1-880692-41-4 (hardcover edition with audio CD)
ISBN 1-880692-43-0 (hardcover edition without audio CD)
ISBN 1-880692-42-2 (trade paperback edition without audio CD)
ISBN 1-880692-44-9 (trade paperback edition with audio CD)

Printed in the United States of America

The song, "Leap of Faith," words and music by Robin Crow and Karen Staley. Copyright 1995 by Crow Notes (BMI) and All Our Town Music/Sony/ATV Songs LLC dba Tree Publishing Co., Inc. (BMI). International Copyright Secured. All Rights Reserved. Used By Permission.

The song, "The Logical Song," words and music by Rick Davies and Roger Hodgson. Copyright 1979 by Almo Music Corp. and Delicate Music. International Copyright Secured. All Rights Reserved. Used By Permission.

The song, "Mercy Street," words and music by Peter Gabriel. Copyright 1986 by Cliofine Ltd/Hidden Pun Music BMI. International Copyright Secured. All Rights Reserved. Used By Permission.

The song, "The Higher I Fly," words and music by Robin Crow and Gary Nicholson. Copyright 1999 by Crow Notes (BMI) and Gary Nicholson Music (ASCAP). International Copyright Secured. All Rights Reserved. Used By Permission.

The song, "You Can't Always Get What You Want," words and music by Mick Jagger and Keith Richards. Worldwide copyright owner ABKCO Music, Inc. International Copyright Secured. All Rights Reserved. Used By Permission.

The song, "A Day In The Life," words and music by John Lennon and Paul McCartney. Copyright 1967 by Northern Songs Ltd. International Copyright Secured. All Rights Reserved. Used By Permission.

The song, "Owner of a Lonely Heart," words and music Trevor Rabin/Jon Anderson/Chris Squire/Trevor Horn. Copyright 1983 Affirmative Music, BMI/Unforgettable Songs, ASCAP. International Copyright Secured. All Rights Reserved. Used By Permission.

The song, "Hotel California," words and music by Don Henley/Glenn Frey/Don Felder. Copyright 1976 Cass County Music/Red Cloud Music/Fingers Music ASCAP. International Copyright Secured. All Rights Reserved. Used By Permission.

The song, "Curious Thing," words and music by Amy Grant and Wayne Kirkpatrick. Copyright 1997 Age To Age Music, Inc. (ASCAP/Careers-BMG Music Publishing, Inc. (BMI)/ Magic Beans Music (BMI)). International Copyright Secured. All Rights Reserved. Used By Permission.

The song, "Gift With A Golden Gun," words and music by David Paich and Bobby Kimball. Copyright 1981 Hudmar Publishing Co., Inc. (ASCAP) and Sheetfire Music (BMI). International Copyright Secured. All Rights Reserved. Used By Permission.

The song, "Man In The Mirror," words and music by Siedah Garrett and Glen Ballard. Copyright 1987 by MCA Music Publishing, A Division of MCA Inc., Aerostation Corporation and Yellowbrick Road Music. Copyright Secured. All Rights Reserved. Used By Permission.

The song, "Another Day In Paradise," words and music by Phil Collins. Copyright 1989 Philip Collins Ltd. (PRS)/Hit and Run Music (Pub) Ltd. (PRS). International Copyright Secured. All Rights Reserved. Used By Permission.

The song, "Turn This World Around," words and music by Keith Thomas, Amy Grant, and Beverly Darnall. Copyright 1997 Sony/ATV Tunes LLC/Yellow Elephant Music, Inc./Age To Age Music (ASCAP)/Annie Merle Music (ASCAP). International Copyright Secured. All Rights Reserved. Used By Permission.

ACKNOWLEDGMENTS

During the year and a half it took to write this book, there was always a whirlwind of activity around me that included recording a new album, overseeing the completion of two more studios at Dark Horse Recording, and embarking on a new album project with Jon Anderson. More importantly, I had the privilege of crossing paths with literally hundreds of people who have made my life a richer experience and who influenced the course of this book. I am deeply grateful to...

- My parents, J. and Patty Kilpatrick, for your amazing support, even when you suspected I was diving into a pool with no water.

- My family at large: Laura Runge; Frank Runge; John Runge; Mark, Beth, Sarah, and Joel Maybee; Virgil and Louise LeQuire; Alan and Andrée LeQuire; Paul, Angelia, and Lauren LeQuire; Lista LeQuire, Kent Wonnell, Dustin, Alden, and Rollin Wonnell; Rollin and Ruth Lasseter; Nancy Brown; Emil, Wesley, and Shelby Crow; Emily Crow; Dawn Crow; Joan Crow; and in loving memory of "Doc," Ruby, and Emil Crow, Sr.

- Mike and Tara Rayburn, for constant encouragement on all fronts, and a special thank you to Mike for using the phrase "jump... and the net will appear." I wrote it down and here's the book!

- My staff... Ed Simonton, Rob Evans, Philip Cooper, and Kevin Gains for running Dark Horse seven days a week and for countless hours recording my projects. Also to Damon Seale and Larry Repasky... for helping us put out all our last-minute fires.

- All the craftsmen and work crews who helped me realize the dream and creation of the <u>new</u> Dark Horse Recording, especially Brent Seaton, Tom Blackburn, Stan Justice, Bobby DeLoach, Jackie DeLoach, Ted and Denise Judy, and Bill (Hatchet Head) Story. We're not done yet—just taking a short break...

- My publisher, David Dunham, and Robert D. Smith and Nancy Rose for showing me the ropes in the new world of publishing.

- My mentor and friend, Philip J. Hickey, for taking me under your wing with great advice and wise counsel.

- Joshua, Geraldine, and Dr. Slack... thanks for supporting me with your time, energy, resources, and debates for 20 years now!

- Bill and Jan Horn... you have stuck with me through thick and thin.

- My friends with whom I've shared many hours in wondrous conversations of philosophical exchange: Terry Wilemon, Ken Wilemon, Jon and Jane Anderson, Gary and Lynne Hedden, Mark Hollingsworth, Carey Dodson, Dave Schober, Chuck Wild, Lindy Rasmussen, and Jim Ingle.

- Clarke Schleicher, Brent King, Ed Simonton, and Eric Elwell for tirelessly engineering my latest album, *Second Nature*; and to Ken Mansfield, Beth Lewis, and Dan Lacey for career wisdom.

- The musicians on *Second Nature*... Steve Brewster, Eric Darken, Paul Brannon, Béla Fleck, Kirk Whalum, Randy Goodrum, Craig Nelson, Gary Lunn, George Tidwell, Sam Levine, Pat Coil, Phil Keaggy, Neil Andrews, Jim Williamson, Ron Guzek, Barbara Bailey Hutchison, Jeff Savage, Jackie Street, and Ken Wilemon. Thanks for bringing my music to life.

- All the producers, musicians, singers, and songwriters who have recorded at Dark Horse during the last six years... you have enriched my life by allowing me to be a part of your music and by giving me the pleasure of spending time with you.

TABLE OF CONTENTS

DEDICATION

To my four fabulous children—Savana, Nakota, Joseph, and Andrew—and to my wife, Nancy, who not only put in countless hours as my silent partner writing this book, but has shown me the deeper path of raising a family.

FOREWORD

When Robin Crow asked me to write the Foreword for his book, *Jump...and the Net Will Appear*, I leaped at the chance. Why? Because I've seen close up his remarkable transformation, and can only hope you'll take time to learn from his journey as well. Interestingly enough, this book began working its magic before it was even published. I was on a cross-country plane trip with manuscript in hand, intending to write this Foreword, when the man sitting next to me asked to read a few pages. Thirty minutes later, I wrestled the book from his grasp as he spilled out his story. "It's incredible! This book is exactly what I needed to read at this moment in my life. I have been tortured whether to start my own business or stay in the safe world of accounting. The answer is now clear to me." What an affirmation!

It seems like almost yesterday that I was riding with Robin in his "concert truck"—an old Ryder loaded down, with balding tires, and with no air conditioning to chase away the Tennessee summer swelter. Robin spoke of his dreams and goals and how he planned to achieve them. Now, realize this was a single guy with a good heart; a national recording artist, but broke—living in a one-bedroom apartment and spinning his wheels. However, the more he shared his dreams, the clearer it became to me that his study of human behavior was about to pay off. Robin had studied success patterns through mentors such as Brian Tracy, Napoleon Hill, Stephen Covey, Tony Robbins and so many more. Now it was his turn.

His formula—have faith, set goals, then JUMP!—started to show results immediately with incredible, positive life changes. Each goal he achieved was replaced by higher, more aggressive goals. Of course, with all my CEO wisdom, I began to caution him to "start playing it safe now." Cheerfully thanking me, while ignoring my advice, Robin would charge off to the next challenge!

Now, you ask, did any of these dreams come true? Let's see: within a few short years, I attended his wedding, held his newborns, listened to his new CDs, and stood on the top floor of a spectacular, world-class, Robin Crow-designed recording studio. *Jump... and the Net Will Appear* is loaded with such true life inspirational stories.

This book is already changing the lives of people who have read it. I will be encouraging the 9,000 people who work in my company's restaurants to read this special work. I encourage you to do the same.

Philip J. Hickey, Jr.
President/Chief Executive Officer
Longhorn Steak Houses/RARE Hospitality, Inc.

INTRODUCTION

Every one of us dreams of a life that is rich with happiness, health, and prosperity. We all believe somewhere deep inside that we have talents to offer that are truly unique; that we are here for a purpose, to make a difference, and to benefit the lives of others. Often our vision for fulfillment and zest for life begins to fade as we get caught up in the frustrations of day to day survival. Our faith gets challenged, our hope to achieve the quality of life we've dreamed of begins to crack, and our dreams shatter into so many pieces we eventually give up trying to put them back together again. But we <u>can</u> break out of these mental chains and find freedom! All of us have the potential to lift up our thoughts, take charge of our lives, and shape our circumstances. *Jump... and the Net Will Appear* is about resisting fear when it tries to make a home in our hearts. It's about finding strength during times of adversity and learning how to create a higher quality of life by using our God-given abilities to turn our dreams into reality! There is a tremendous transformation in making this discovery. It is a distinction which empowers us to experience all that life has to offer... to take charge of our destiny... to bring forth our unique and individual talents to the world: To make a difference.

Since the fourth grade I have lived, breathed, and slept music. I love everything about the music business: writing new songs, all–night recording sessions, interviews, packing, rehearsing... wandering through strange cities, all-night drives on the bus, asking directions, making friends, strange hotels... hanging out in airports, hanging out backstage... waiting for the show to begin, and then the pay-off—performing my heart out in concert!

For years I bet everything I had on the hopes of making it big as a recording artist. I've appeared on national television many times and performed almost 2,000 concerts, building a career with a philosophy of touring hard and never giving up. To date, I have recorded six albums, and, as of this writing, am completing my seventh.

But music is not my only passion. I have also devoted much of my life to understanding what drives human behavior. I have observed many people who have overcome all kinds of difficult challenges and hardships. These are people whose perseverance has become a source of strength... a source of empowering beliefs.

What inspires one person to high levels of personal and professional success while others don't even begin to tap into their potential? Why is it that two people with similar circumstances will have two entirely different outlooks on life? Why does one person have so much passion for life that he gets up early and stays up late to pursue his dreams while the other finds it difficult to even get out of bed without complaining? There came a point in my own life when I felt I had accomplished so much, yet my life was spinning out of control. I was like a jet airplane sailing down the runway at 115 miles per hour when 120 is needed to gain air speed, lift off, and then fly. I realized that it didn't matter if the runway was 100 miles long, without that extra burst of power I was never going to fly. I was like a car running on five cylinders instead of eight. I was getting down the road, but it was a struggle.

Then I began asking questions such as:

- *How can I have a deeper and richer life experience?*
- *What are my core values and beliefs?*
- *Can I have a successful career, wealth, and a rich family life?*
- *Is it possible to achieve these things while remaining spiritually balanced?*

Discovering the answers to these questions has completely turned my life around. But it took a long time to learn some of these simple lessons—it seemed as if I learned most the hardest possible way. After twenty years of hard work I was still living hand-to-mouth. Often I was making $3,000 a night to perform a 90-minute concert and yet was stuck on what seemed to be an endless treadmill in a career that demands 1,000 percent at all times to keep up. The illusion of show business is deceiving from afar. I've known many artists who were in the national spotlight with songs on the *Billboard* charts and yet, because of the enormous overhead to keep a national career going, these people would be out on the street in a month if they quit touring. That's how it was for me... lawyers, accountants, road crew, trucks, sound systems, light systems, managers, agents, and my own office and personal assistant kept me in the poor house. Something had to give...

- **The road I had chosen was no longer making sense...**
  - **I was tired of traveling through life without a roadmap...**
    - **In everyone's life, it all comes down to one defining moment and this was mine...**
      - **I made a commitment to designing my life and setting goals for my future...**
        - **I immediately began to take action toward making my dreams come true...**

I jumped . . .

Once and for all I stopped being influenced by the nay-sayers of the world. I was through with being influenced by other people's limited systems of beliefs. I was unwilling to settle for less than the best I could be. Now armed with a solid vision for achieving a life of abundance for my family and me, I had a strong sense of purpose which compelled me to find ways to overcome obstacles that used to stop me cold in my tracks. By setting goals and gaining clarity on desired outcomes for my life—emotionally, physically, and financially— I started down a path that has brought a life of abundance greater than anything I could have imagined just five years ago.

Perhaps many of the changes I'm talking about are subjective, but the massive change in my finances is not. Almost overnight I began amassing wealth beyond what I had thought possible. And... while climbing the mountain of financial independence, I have been having the time of my life! I took my small home recording studio and began to expand, creating a world-class complex on my ten-acre farm in Franklin, Tennessee. Dark Horse Recording has become a haven that attracts some of the world's most outstanding pop, Christian, and country stars, such as Wynonna, Dolly Parton, Neil Diamond, John Hiatt, Faith Hill, and Amy Grant... as well as a place to work on my own music. I signed with a new record label and am planning new tours, television appearances, and other adventures that are just around the corner. All this happened because I learned how to tap into hidden potential and strength that I didn't even know I had. That awakening has brought about positive change for my entire family. As a husband and father of four, raising a family has been a path of spiritual growth with amazing challenges and blessings. We have discovered that a positive attitude of unlimited possibilities has brought us overwhelming happiness and led us down the road to deeper fulfillment. Like a seed soon to bring forth new life, the future has become an exciting journey full of wondrous possibilities!

Think about it... if humans are the only creatures on the planet that have total control over their thoughts, surely we can use this same power not only for our benefit, but for the benefit of those around us. And... all this will be reflected in our service, our compassion for others, and our giving back to the local and global communities.

As the title *Jump... and the Net Will Appear* suggests, this book is about taking risks and learning to embrace the unknown. My motto has always been, "A ship is safe in the harbor, but that's not what ships are built for." These are my stories. Some are humorous, and all of them are inspiring accounts of persistence, determination, and growth. This book is a wake-up call for anyone who is on a quest for a deeper and more meaningful life experience... who doesn't want to ever settle for less than the best life has to offer.

So don't be afraid to follow your heart...
and if you're willing to jump...
your net will appear.

1

THE POWER OF THOUGHT

Tonight your life will change forever
once you understand the
POWER OF THOUGHT

You'll grow rich beyond your wildest dreams
When you mix powerful thoughts
With persistence and burning desire
There are no boundaries to what you might achieve
When your thoughts begin to spark…
And ignite into a blazing fire
Your life will change forever once you understand the
POWER OF THOUGHT

All the castles that have ever been built
All the great pyramids ever made
Began as a pure and simple seed of thought
Long before any plan was laid
Your life will change forever once you understand the
POWER OF THOUGHT

Now let me bring to light one of God's beautiful truths
Your thoughts are the mirror to your very soul
They are the choreographers of all life's dances
And the shaper of your circumstances
Your life will change forever once you understand the
POWER OF THOUGHT

Every song, every poem, and every dream
Was formed by an idea someone created
Remember... everything we do and all that's ever been said
Started as a thought in somebody's head
Your life will change forever once you understand the
POWER OF THOUGHT

More gold has been mined from the thoughts of men
Than has ever been taken from the ground
More wealth has come from great ideas
Than any buried treasure that's ever been found
Your life will change forever once you understand the
POWER OF THOUGHT

So choose your thoughts with care
For they will set your course in motion
Let them lift your spirit to catch the wind
Let your highest dreams set sail across life's ocean
Your life will change forever once you understand the
POWER OF THOUGHT

So remember... our character is the complete
Sum of all our thoughts
And it's our choice... to think in the positive from now on
Because if we have the will to change and
The heart to persevere

There's no limit to how far we can go from here
Your life will change forever once you understand the
POWER OF THOUGHT

"Power of Thought"
lyrics by Robin Crow

*The success we achieve
will always be in
direct proportion to the
risks we are willing to take.*

Robin Crow

2

LEAP OF FAITH

When I was a child,
I dreamed I could fly like the wind
Time after time after time,
I would spread my wings and pretend
As the years went by, I settled for less
But the time has come to put it to the test
It takes a leap of faith,
When the moment of truth arrives
It takes a leap of faith, to truly believe I will fly
I know the further I climb, the further I may fall
But this time I'm risking it all

"Leap Of Faith"
lyrics by Robin Crow & Karen Staley

Let's get right down to it. This is not a book about living life as a gambler going off on hare-brained, get-rich-quick schemes, jumping blindly into relationships, or conjuring up half-cocked business deals. It is a book about overcoming fear and developing the courage to take risks in all aspects of our lives. Once people are willing to walk away from old patterns, their lives can change drastically.

- ◆ It's taking a risk to recommit to a difficult relationship.
- ◆ It's taking a risk to tell someone you love them.
- ◆ It's taking a risk to raise children.
- ◆ It's taking a risk to commit to a better diet or exercise.
- ◆ It's taking a risk to lay it on the line and immerse yourself in the career that you love.

Most of us are fearful of taking risks to one degree or another because risk-taking opens up the possibility of failure, but together we can learn to overcome those fears that keep us from achieving our dreams. Together we can *Jump... and Our Net Will Appear*.

Change your thoughts and
you change your world.
—Dr. Norman Vincent Peale

Like A Ship

A ship is safe in the harbor,
but that's not what ships are built for.

The day I left high school I set out in pursuit of a life in the music industry, lured by the temptation of fame and fortune. I was low on talent, but high on enthusiasm. I was clueless, but determined. I was ignorant, but persistent. I was caught up in the chase and the quest for success, but I was like a ship without a rudder to guide me on a steady course. I did not have the understanding of the importance of self-improvement in all areas to balance out my life. I didn't understand the importance of physical health: that I would not only look and feel better, but I would also have the additional fuel to go the extra mile each day. Nor did I understand how important it is to have a positive attitude toward all people and all situations. **I simply thought if I was the fastest and loudest guitar player all these other things would take care of themselves!** I have since learned that it doesn't matter how much wind you have in your sails. If your life is incomplete and unbalanced, sailing fast will probably mean sailing off course. For many years that's what my life was like. I worked as hard as anyone, expending energy in all kinds of ways, counting on success to bring me happiness, but there was always an underlying conflict in my life. Over time I began to understand that it was far more important to achieve personal success than professional success. I learned that I can change my thoughts, which can change my behavior, which can change my life—and thereby enrich the lives of others. But it didn't happen overnight.

Learning To Learn

...they sent me away to teach me how to be sensible,
logical, responsible, practical.
And they showed me a world where I could be so
dependable, clinical, intellectual, cynical.
At night, when all the world's asleep,
the questions run so deep for such a simple man.
"The Logical Song"
lyrics by Rick Davies and Roger Hodgson
(Supertramp)

When I was in high school, if you had told me that at age forty-five I would have become a perpetual student, someone who loved to learn, I would have said you were crazy. As a teenager I hated school and made poor grades... learning was a four-letter word to me. I didn't see the point of memorizing facts and figures that were of no interest to me. How were they going to apply to my life? After all, I wanted to be a recording artist. What did knowledge and learning have to do with that? Of course, that kind of thinking was my first and biggest mistake. Learning more about the industry and learning how others before me worked their way through the ranks could have saved me years of hardship and struggle. But I have changed. I have gone from someone who hated the idea of learning something new, to someone who loves to learn. I have become a perpetual student. My favorite pastime is spending an hour in the self-help or business aisle at the book store. Discovering new distinctions that can improve my quality of life has become a treasure hunt.

Never Give Up

No matter what you've been through, no matter how many times you've stumbled, today can be the mark of new beginnings, the day your life takes a new direction toward total abundance. **By lifting my thoughts and learning to focus on the unlimited things I have to be grateful for,** I went from someone who believed the world was conspiring to keep me down to someone who believed the world was conspiring to help me succeed. That change in attitude can make all the difference in your life. As peak performance coach Tony Robbins says,

"The past does not equal the future," and he's right. My own life is testimony to this. I stumbled and failed hundreds of times, but I never gave up. It seems that every success I've had in my life has come at the time when defeat was on the verge of taking over. This has taught me to keep on keeping on even during the hardest of times. It also taught me how to turn defeat into stepping stones of opportunity.

Dreams into Reality

Looking on empty streets, all she can see
Are the dreams all made solid
Are the dreams made real
All of the buildings, all of those cars
Were once just a dream
In somebody's head

"Mercy Street"
lyrics by Peter Gabriel

The fact that you are reading this book tells me that you are the kind of person who is interested in getting the most out of life... you are a person who is still dreaming. As long as you keep on dreaming there are simply no limits to what you can achieve in your life. With an attitude of endless possibilities, life becomes an exciting journey with adventures and uncharted territories just waiting to be discovered. For better or worse, I have always lived life on my own terms. It seems I've learned every lesson the hardest possible way, but in the long run this has helped shape my character and therefore my confidence for the positive. All my life, people accused me of being a dreamer. And they were right. It took a while, but once I married those dreams with the ingredients of success...

♦ *a clear sense of direction*
♦ *setting goals*
♦ *willingness to change old patterns*
♦ *burning desire*
♦ *willingness to take action*
♦ *positive mental attitude*
♦ *persistence*
♦ *faith*

. . . I discovered the world *really is* conspiring to make me successful. Anything is possible as long as you hold on to your dreams, step out in faith, and back it up with determination and persistence.

The Higher We Fly

Flying high is not always the safest place; in fact it stands to reason that the higher we fly, the further we may fall. The risk is always greater when we're in unknown territory, but the potential rewards are almost infinite. We all dream of fearlessly taking flight to heights of greatness with our aspirations. But often people settle for life on the ground, operating far below their potential for success and happiness.

*Instead of spinning the dials of life hoping for a lucky
break, as if you were playing a slot machine,
you must instead study and emulate those
who have already done what you want to do
and achieved the results you want to achieve.*

—Brian Tracy

It is second nature to persevere even when we face adversity. It is second nature to want to strive for a richer life experience. It is second nature to dream of a life full of abundance. All this is available to everyone who is willing to lift up his thoughts and face his fears... willing to put one foot in front of the other and persist. When defeat overtakes us, the easiest and most logical thing to do is to quit, but that's when we have the greatest opportunity to excel. That's when we can turn the corner and achieve a higher standard in our lives.

> *I learned how to struggle*
> *Had to fight to get by*
> *I practiced resistance*
> *With all of my might*
> *Now there's a mountain before me*
> *I'm determined to climb*
> *Although the distance is great*
> *I'll make it this time*
> "The Higher I Fly"
> lyrics by Robin Crow and Gary Nicholson

Living in the Flow of Abundance

We can't walk crooked and think straight.
—*Stephen R. Covey*

Living in the flow of abundance is about focusing on what you can give instead of what you can get. Perhaps the best definition of abundance is success, both in accumulating material wealth and in maintaining a deep-rooted desire to contribute. There are spiritual principles that apply to everyone without prejudice. Your business life and your spiritual life should go hand in hand. Your spiritual life should be reflected in the way you run your business, the way you treat those with whom you work, and the way you treat your competitors. It goes without saying that honesty and integrity are fundamental ingredients for earning the respect of others.

Searching For Happiness

> *If you help people get what they want,*
> *then you'll get what you want.*
>
> —*Zig Ziglar*

> *You can't always get what you want,*
> *But sometimes you just might find*
> *You get what you need*
>
> *"You Can't Always Get What You Want"*
> *lyrics by Mick Jagger & Keith Richards*
> *(The Rolling Stones)*

Happiness comes from spiritual abundance, not from material abundance. It's not hard to measure someone's material wealth, but to gauge spiritual wealth we have to look at our lives. How do we value our life and the lives of others? What are the depths of our relationships? Have we used the gifts we've been given for the good of others as well as ourselves? How well do we practice love? Mother Teresa said that the greatest poverty was spiritual, not physical. Happiness is not a by-product of circumstances, but rather a spiritual principle and practice that we can tap into regardless of outer circumstances.

We live in a culture that teaches us to raise our standards for "happiness" at every turn as we move through life. Think about it: hundreds of times every day we are bombarded with advertisers telling us—or brainwashing us—that if we wear the right clothes, use the right shampoo, drive the right car, or associate with the right people, we will be happy.

I read the news today oh boy
Four thousand holes in Blackburn, Lancashire
And though the holes were rather small
They had to count them all
Now they know how many holes
It takes to fill the Albert Hall.
I'd love to turn you on
"A Day In The Life"
lyrics by John Lennon & Paul McCartney
(Beatles)

For example, when we strike out on our own we buy our first television set with a 15-inch screen, and it gives us a good feeling for a while. Over time we discover that it no longer satisfies our demand for quality... we have now raised our standard for what is acceptable. So we set our sights on a bigger and more expensive television that meets our current definition of top quality. This time it's a 27-inch with a higher quality picture and better sound. For a while it seems like this is as good as it gets. But then we start asking ourselves, "What if I had a high definition big screen television... what if I had a DVD player... what if I had a surround sound system? That will make me feel even better." But even all that's not enough, because in a short while we'll realize we need one for the bedroom; and we start the process all over again. These things provide only a brief illusion of happiness. Material possessions may provide a sense of comfort and security, but they will never bring any kind of lasting happiness.

It is second nature to thirst for a full and rewarding life, yet often we end up looking in the wrong places to quench our thirst. If our quest for material wealth is based on what we can get instead of what we can give, then we will be left with emptiness in our lives. After the high has worn off from our endless acquisition of outer pleasures, then what? If we don't develop a plan to take control of our lives, others are standing by to do it for us. When we learn to change our inner world, our outer world will then begin to change.

> *Remember, no more effort is required*
> *to aim high in life,*
> *to demand abundance and prosperity,*
> *than is required to accept misery and poverty.*
> —*Napoleon Hill*

Take courage: if you feel you're being called to venture out and take on new challenges, remember that we all have the ability not only to survive but also to prosper. We were created by God, with the possibility to experience a fulfilling and satisfying life, and there is no reason why we should settle for less than a life of excellence and abundance.

> *I just took the energy it takes to pout*
> *and wrote some blues.*
> —*Duke Ellington*

3

GOING SOLO

*Only one thing is more important than
learning from experience,
and that is not learning from experience.*
—*Sir John M. Templeton*

In the early sixties, life was simple and predictable
growing up in Fort Worth, Texas. In many ways, it was
the best of times in America. There was a sense of
prosperity and hope, and it was all personified in our
youthful president, John F. Kennedy. He was not only
good-looking and charismatic, but he was also a man
with a deep love for this country. He exemplified these
qualities through his unwavering leadership. On November 22, 1963, the nation went into shock when he was
assassinated. It was hard to believe something like this
could happen. In an instant, he was gone. Earlier that
day, the president was in Fort Worth giving a speech.
Quite a few of my classmates had gone downtown to see
him. He then headed to Dallas, where, at approximately
12:30 in the afternoon, he was slain. It was horrible and
unforgettable as I watched some of my teachers weeping,
right in front of the class.

Then it was 1964. That was the year the Ford Mustang first appeared, and my father—who has always been somewhat of a car buff—bought one. I later learned that the creation of this car was a turning point in the life of Lee Iacocca, a young Ford executive who believed strongly that the time was ripe for a car that would appeal to the younger generation. The enormous success of the Mustang rocketed him into the position of president of Ford Motors. Iacocca had tapped into the spirit of an optimistic generation.

> *We were young and cocky.*
> *We saw ourselves as artists,*
> *about to produce the finest masterpieces*
> *the world had ever seen.*
> —Lee Iacocca

It was a time when we were shooting men into outer space, and Martin Luther King, Jr. was leading a non-violent march for civil rights—a cause that earned him the Nobel Peace Prize.

There was a fresh breeze blowing across America. Anything seemed possible. And then something happened that set in motion a fever from coast to coast... our pop culture was about to be changed forever. Beatlemania had arrived!

It was a Sunday evening at my grandparents' home. I'll never forget watching the Beatles perform "I Want To Hold Your Hand" as they made their debut on *The Ed Sullivan Show*. There they were in black and white... John, George, Paul, and Ringo. Wow! "Listen to that music... look at those screaming girls... check out that hair!" I was hooked! I knew right then and there, that was the life for me. There was no turning back. The lights... the music... the screaming fans. What an exciting life I could have if I could sing and play guitar. It all seemed so clear—this was my destiny! Of course, about five million other kids were thinking the same thing.

In 1964 the Beatles landed on American soil, and nothing in my life has been the same since!

The first thing I did was build a microphone stand out of my Erector set. I managed to get a five-dollar Radio Shack microphone and taped it to the top. The thing would barely stand up, but it didn't really matter. It was my first piece of gear, and now I was in show business! At age eleven, I had chosen my path... I was a man on a mission (okay, a boy on a mission) with a vision in my head that was so strong it guided and shaped my destiny for the next twenty-five years.

From time to time my folks would go out for the evening and hire a sitter for my sister and me. Guess what? She brought a guitar and a chord book! One evening I picked up her guitar and learned every chord in that book. My love affair with the guitar had begun. Soon I had talked my parents into buying me my own guitar. For hours I would strum the chords I knew, trying to see how fast I could move my hands from one position to the next. Before long I was playing dozens of Beatle songs and starting to write a few of my own. One day I decided it was time to stand up as I played, but I didn't have a guitar strap. Undaunted, I took a few nails, bashed them into my poor red acoustic guitar, got a belt, hooked it on, and was on my way. I began to play in talent shows and spent hours with my friends learning songs by the Dave Clark Five, Herman's Hermits, and the Beatles.

Big shots are only little shots
who keep shooting.

—*Harvey Mackay*

Then I graduated—from elementary school—and moved on to junior high. That's when I joined a band called the Agitators. We were all seventh-graders. To this day, it is one of my favorite names for a band. We played at school dances and private parties for twenty dollars. That wasn't bad for those days—about five bucks apiece. Of course, back then our touring costs were extremely low. I would throw my guitar and amplifier into the trunk of my mother's car, and we were off to the big gig... perhaps someone's birthday party or the back of a flatbed truck at a Shriners parade. We had no manager, no agent, no accountants, no lawyers, and no record company telling us they still didn't hear a radio hit. Come to think of it, it was great!

Of course, a really good rock-and-roll band never seems to last very long. Soon each member becomes convinced he is the star of the show and takes off to do his own solo project. By the eighth grade, the Agitators had reached their artistic climax, which put each of us into a fragile and delicate state. At a time when we could have become a global phenomenon, it was evident we needed to explore our artistic range and concentrate on other aspects of school life such as *finding girlfriends!*

I have always wondered which events, moments, or distinctions cause a person to make choices that alter the course of his life. There were three thousand of us in high school and, looking back, I can see how different events were beginning to shape our futures.

A man's mind may be likened to a garden,
which may be intelligently cultivated
or allowed to run wild.

—*James Allen*

As for me... my mind was running wild with visions of grandeur. I was certain I wanted to pursue a life as a pop star. After all, I was writing my own songs, influenced by Jimi Hendrix, Eric Clapton, and a new British group called Yes. By the time I was in the eighth grade I was in a new band and we were writing our own music together. We rehearsed constantly and took ourselves seriously. To this day each one of us is still playing music professionally, and I've often wondered what would have happened if we'd stayed together all these years. As time went on, my other friends who were serious musicians headed on to college to learn music theory and composition and to study jazz. As for me, I was hell-bent on getting as far away from school as possible. I managed to land a full-time position in a group called Great Expectations (sounds like a dating service). We played the nightclub circuit around Texas and Louisiana. We wore ridiculous matching jumpsuits and played top forty songs that sounded even more ridiculous. Back then my goal was to be a traveling musician, so as far as I was concerned I had hit the big time... $150 a week! Just when I thought I was going straight to the top—no one can stop me now!—I got fired! This was the moment of truth: it was time to go solo!

Perhaps I had already learned my first lessons in personal achievement:

♦ *I was motivated to take control of my destiny.*

♦ *I had a burning desire*
♦ *I had a plan*
♦ *I was focused*
♦ *And I began taking action.*

Developing as a solo performer was a long, uphill climb. If you happened to visit Fort Worth about twenty-five years ago and stumbled into a disgusting hole-in-the-wall dive covered with the stench of beer, there was a good chance I was playing there. I played any and everywhere that people would listen. Pretty soon it became obvious that it was time to branch out, so I headed thirty miles east to Dallas where I set up home in a small one-room apartment overlooking a freeway. My apartment, food, and gas expenses came to almost $250 a month, which was terrifying at the time. I called every talent agent in the phone book, looking for work. Eventually, one of them got me an audition at a huge Japanese restaurant called the Royal Tokyo, which was still under construction.

Here's proof that musicians are willing to do almost anything to be heard. For my audition, I set up my sound system in the middle of the construction site and performed for twenty minutes. The Japanese investors had the entire crew stop working to come and listen. It was right beside a major freeway (not to be confused with the one that almost ran through my apartment), and the roof wasn't even completed. What a ridiculous sight—me playing American pop songs for a half dozen men who could barely speak English!

After that humiliating experience I returned to my new home and soon forgot about the whole thing. But guess what? Six months later they called me up. I had the job!

♦ *Because I was willing to do what others were not I had gotten my first steady paying job as a solo guitarist.*

♦ *Taking the risk of embarrassment had paid off!*

♦ *Once again I was learning early lessons in personal achievement.*

For six months I played at the Royal Tokyo, five hours each night. They would have kept me there forever if I had wanted to stay. By the time I left, my musical abilities had really improved, and I had developed quite a taste for Japanese cuisine. Once again I was ready to expand my horizons and move on. With the little money I had saved, I hit the road with a van full of gear and headed up to Colorado to play ski resorts. I didn't have any engagements lined up, so once I arrived I took a job working as a ranch hand at a guest ranch way off the beaten path, aptly called Lost Valley Ranch. On my days off I would drive a couple of hundred miles into Denver and knock on the doors of every booking agent listed in the phone book. Upon on hearing me play, a few agents set up auditions for me. Once again, I would go to great lengths—sometimes driving hundreds of miles—just to set up in some club and perform a few songs for the manager. But before long it paid off. I quit my job on the ranch and took off for Crested Butte, Montana—my first steady gig. I remember crossing the treacherous Monarch Pass, where I pulled off the road and went to sleep in my van to wait out a snow storm. When I awoke my body was shivering and shaking so hard from the cold that I could barely function. My van was encased by a three-foot layer of snow. Not only was I unprepared, but I had no idea of the potential danger of the situation

I had put myself in. Little did I know that twenty years later I would have another brush with death while attempting to drive over that same pass on a seventeen-mile stretch of black ice.

Playing ski resorts was great. For a nineteen-year-old kid, getting paid to hang out with the beautiful and rich was a dream. For my kind of music they were above-average audiences and enjoyed listening to my compositions. But all too soon winter turned into spring, ski season came to a close, and I was out of work again. I've had a love affair with Colorado ever since, returning many times to play at the mountain resorts and then at some of the colleges and universities. Later, I had the privilege to perform at Red Rocks Amphitheater in front of almost 10,000 people. Now that's a Rocky Mountain high!

> *For the things we have to learn before*
> *we can do them,*
> *we learn by doing them.*
> *—Aristotle*

During the following year I performed in all kinds of situations. I was even asked to play guitar in a rock musical version of Shakespeare's "A Midsummer Night's Dream" in Chicago. During the three months the show ran, I was introduced to many aspects of theater. It was a well-produced musical with a large cast of actors, dancers, sound and lighting technicians, and, of course, other musicians. It was my first exposure to true professionalism in the entertainment industry. There were producers, writers, and investors all hoping the play would be such a big hit that they would soon be heading to Broadway. From this experience I developed a passion for combining theatrical lighting and stage sets with my music. But before any of that was to come to pass, I decided to put together my own band. We paid our dues on the Holiday Inn circuit (the kiss of death for any aspiring musician). If you're not careful, playing the lounges can cause musical rigor mortis to set in.

We kept a strict rehearsal schedule, writing and rehearsing every day. At some hotels the only time they would allow us to rehearse was after hours, which meant as soon as we finished the last set of the night, around 2:00 a.m., we would begin rehearsing, sometimes until the sun came up. Then we would finally go to our rooms to sleep. Needless to say, this was not our idea of fun, and I began looking for some way to move out of the clubs and begin playing concerts. It was time to move to Los Angeles and try our luck there.

The day we arrived I was looking through the phone book under "Theatrical Agencies" and saw a listing for the National School Assemblies Agency. It was obvious after one phone call that an opportunity had presented itself for playing concerts. You know what they say, "Be careful what you ask for; you just might get it." Within a week we had auditioned and were back out on the road performing. It was total overload: a test of endurance and stamina.

We were hitting as many as three high schools a day, each in a different town. Although our schedule had been planned with precision, each day was a race to see if we could pull it off at breakneck speed. It was actually a great opportunity to cut my teeth as a performer in front of large crowds. Many times we were playing in front of two to three thousand students. We lived like true gypsies. I had purchased an old U-Haul truck and built a camper in the front half. It had tiny two-foot-wide bunk beds and a wraparound couch. It had an icebox that—you guessed it—ran on a block of ice. That's where the three of us slept, ate, and lived... our home on wheels. It looked and ran like it was on its last leg. If we could get through an entire week without a breakdown, we were doing well. It would have been perfect for attending Grateful Dead concerts.

We were the personification of the *band on the run.* Every day we would wake up at five in the morning, having already parked the night before alongside the school where we were scheduled to perform. The early morning custodian would unlock the auditorium or gym for us to begin setting up our gear. Once all the heavy lifting was done and we had everything in place, we would head down to the locker room for our daily shower. Many times the football team was having an early morning practice, so there we'd be, three guys who were trying to be rock stars showering with the Snake River Bears or the Flagstaff Warriors. We made a game of giving every shower at each school a rating. Some would have only cold water and a few had only scalding hot water. Some had almost no water pressure, while others only operated at Mach 5, shooting water out with so much force that you couldn't stand in front it. Then there were those showers that would shoot out one tiny stream of water, which would have been fine if you wanted to wash only your little finger.

Around 8:00 a.m. the bell would ring, a couple thousand students would come rushing in, and we would kick off the day with our own brand of rock and roll. They loved us! But that's not saying we were necessarily the greatest. We were playing in front of the entertainment-deprived. The National School Assemblies had about sixty acts roaming the country playing small towns. Most of the performers were guys who had a traveling snake show, or immigrant folk dancers from Austria, or some wannabe poet reciting Longfellow. There was even a husband and wife team who had an archery show. Believe it or not, he would shoot a ping pong ball off the top of his wife's head from across the room with a bow and arrow! Now would your wife let you do that? It was gratifying, however, to be mistaken sometimes for big rock stars. One time while we were setting up, a girl came up and asked Ken Wilemon—my life-long friend and drummer—who we were. He answered, "The Beatles." She replied, "Really?" and then walked away with a satisfied smile on her face.

With the help of a dozen students we would load up the truck, and in an hour's time drive fifty miles to town number two, where we would pull up to the auditorium door. There would be another dozen students ready to sling all that gear onto the stage, and in twenty minutes the bell would ring, students would rush in, and we would start playing. An hour later we would hit the final chord and, at almost lightning speed, load up again. I would get directions to the next school, and by three o'clock in the afternoon, we had performed yet a third concert. Then we would head to the town scheduled for the following morning and find a grocery store for food and our daily block of ice. By now it would be early evening, so we would track down the school and ask if it was possible to get in the night before so we could set up and rehearse. We had a portable two-burner stove and sometimes, in below-freezing weather, we would huddle together in our little camper around our tiny table where we would cook and warm ourselves at the same time. We would then heat up a couple of pots of water, go outside, and wash our dishes. Around midnight we would bed down for five or six hours, get up the next morning, and do it all over again.

It was rock-and-roll boot camp. It made us strong. We learned how to accomplish feats we thought couldn't be done. We learned, for instance, how to set up a couple of thousand pounds of musical equipment in just minutes instead of hours. We learned that we could achieve things like pulling off fifteen concerts a week, a feat that in the beginning seemed impossible. Incredibly, within two years we had performed at almost six hundred schools.

We had boundless energy!

At 22 years old I felt I was already brimming over with experience and now felt confident to make the big move to Hollywood... this time to stay.

4

YES!

Prove yourself
You are the move you make
Take your chances win or loser...
Be yourself
Give your free will a chance
You've got to want to succeed...
Look before you leap
And don't you hesitate at all — No No
"Owner of a Lonely Heart"
lyrics by Rabin/Anderson/Squire/Horn
(Yes)

Yes is one of the most extraordinary pop-rock bands of all time. Since the late sixties they have endured three decades of trends, critics, and the public's fickleness. They have been my musical heroes since I was a teenager.

I remember hearing Yes for the first time during my last year of high school. I was awestruck. Those high, angelic harmonies against the backdrop of their avant-garde approach to rock music was unlike anything I had heard before. The following year Atlantic Records released their album, *Fragile*, which included the classic six-minute hit "Roundabout." I was hooked. I spent hours sitting between my stereo speakers entranced by the majesty and wonder of that album. It was a magical adventure and a musical awakening.

At the same time that the Rolling Stones and Led Zeppelin were pushing the boundaries of vulgarity and sexuality in their concerts and on their records, Yes took the higher road. Their music was textured with complex classical motifs and crafted into high-energy rock. It was the most inspiring music I had ever heard, and I became their biggest fan. Many other bands imitated them, but to this day no other group of musicians has even come close to capturing lightning in a bottle the way Yes did, and still does. Their musical craftsmanship was of a higher caliber than the norm. They were simply in a league of their own. For musicians in my generation, they became the standard by which all other bands were measured.

I wasn't alone in my feelings. Not only were they popular on radio, but every aspiring musician I knew tried to emulate them. In fact, the term "progressive rock" was coined to describe their music. Each player in Yes was a virtuoso in his own right, and when all that extraordinary talent was combined and fused together, the effect was no less than awesome.

The creative force of this legendary band was lead singer and co-writer Jon Anderson, a man who possessed a clear, high voice, unlike any I have heard to this day. His uplifting lyrics blended philosophical and spiritual ideas, which took the band's already amazing music to even higher levels. As I was developing and maturing as a guitarist and songwriter, it was his creativity and positive approach to melody and lyrics that was my greatest influence. In my dreams I fantasized that some-day I would meet and play guitar with Jon Anderson.

It is difficult to say what is impossible,
for the dream of yesterday
is the hope of today
and the reality of tomorrow.
—Robert H. Goddard

This is the story of how our paths crossed, and how I learned the value of seizing the moment and embracing opportunity before it passes by. Sometimes an opportunity presents itself only once, and if you're willing to risk rejection and jump out on a leap of faith, you can change the course of your life.

A Concert of a Lifetime

The first time I ever saw Yes in concert was in front of 55,000 people at Anaheim Stadium, just outside Los Angeles. It was the summer of 1975, and I had just moved to LA after finishing up the National School Assemblies tour of almost 600 high schools in two years. That summer I stayed with friends in North Hollywood. When I heard that Yes was coming to Southern California, I was ecstatic. It was to be an all-day event starting with the classic rock group Gentle Giant, then Gary Wright who had a new hit on the charts called "Dream Weaver," followed by Peter Frampton who was riding the crest of a wave with his mega-hit album *Frampton Comes Alive.*

And then the main event—Yes.

The concert was set up as festival seating, which means there are no reserved seats. Whoever shows up first gets the best shot at sitting up close. I arrived at the stadium the evening before, figuring I would be one of the first in line. Was I ever surprised when I discovered there were already thousands of people who had arrived before me, also prepared to stay the night. By midnight there must have been at least ten thousand fans already spread out on the pavement, creating a seemingly endless river of people as the huge line wove its way through the mammoth stadium parking lot. A thick fog had now set in, which added an eerie glow to the parking lot lights. It was a surreal experience to spend the night with all those people, but nothing compared to the crush of bodies flooding into the stadium once the gates opened the next morning. Tens of thousands rushed onto the open field as everyone claimed a small patch of ground, about one or two square feet, to call his own. There was no room to move. It was an unbelievable sea of humanity.

It seemed like forever waiting for the music to begin, but finally around noon Gentle Giant took to the stage and gave a jaw-dropping performance. Next Gary Wright came on, followed by Peter Frampton who rattled off all his hit songs to the crowd's delight. It was a wonderful afternoon of music, but that's not what I had come for. The long-awaited moment arrived. At last it was time for Yes. The sun was just setting over the stadium when the towering stacks of speakers erupted with Stravinsky's *Firebird Suite*. The giant stage set came alive as hundreds of spotlights began firing to the rhythm of the music. Then thousands of flashing cameras from the audience began to answer back as if engaging in extra-terrestrial conversation. Four powerful laser beams appeared from behind the drums and stretched across the stadium as the audience exploded with applause. You could feel the collective electricity. With chills running down my spine, I remember thinking, "My goodness, this is incredible, and Yes isn't even out here yet!"

As the five band members came out onto the stage, the cheer from 55,000 ecstatic Yes fans was deafening. Jon Anderson was wearing a long white robe, the perfect compliment to his voice and lyrics. When they kicked in with their first song, I was absolutely mesmerized. "Hands down this is the best band in the world," I thought, and that night there was a stadium full of enthusiastic people who agreed with me! In one sense, it was five of the most incredible musicians anyone could possibly imagine, totally in sync and "in their groove." On the other hand, it was clearly Jon's band. As I watched and listened, I thought to myself, "What if someday I could actually meet him? What if I could actually play music with him? What if I could record an album with him?" The idea seemed much too far-fetched to entertain seriously.

That night, time stood still as I took it all in. I've since been to countless concerts, but never has one compared to spending the evening with Yes on that summer night in 1975.

Face to Face

A decade later, Yes was still going strong. In fact, the group had restructured its personnel and resurfaced sounding even better than ever. With the release of the smash hit "Owner of a Lonely Heart," they had captured a new generation of fans and joined a very select group of '70s arena rock acts whose popularity spanned into the '80s. Jon's voice was sounding better than ever, and their new songs reflected the high-tech sounds and current trends. But unlike so many other groups on the charts, Yes's music still had the same depth and substance as before.

By this time, my career as a recording artist had started to blossom. I now had four national albums under my belt and was living in Nashville. I primarily toured college and university campuses and several times my schedule intersected with Yes's, giving me the chance to see them in various cities. In February 1988, I learned that they were coming to the downtown arena in Nashville. As it turned out, I was going to be in town on that very day. Like thousands of other Yes fans, I bought my tickets, anxious for another chance to see them again and hear them perform their latest works.

Finally the day of the concert arrived. I could not stop thinking about how incredible it would be if somehow I could meet with Jon Anderson. "What if I could play him some of my music? What if he liked it? What if somehow, someday we could actually work together?"

It was a fantasy I kept to myself most of the time. It seemed too impossible and too far from my reach. After all, they lived across the ocean, and they were touring and playing internationally. At that time my concert travels were confined to the United States and Canada. It all seemed totally unrealistic.

Just before heading out the door to the concert, I phoned Mark Hollingsworth, a friend and fellow Yes fan. I confessed to him how frustrated I felt being so close and yet so far from meeting Jon. He really encouraged me to make the effort, even at the expense of looking foolish. Mark is a consultant in the music industry, and reminded me of how he had met some other major acts by simply tracking them down backstage; high profile performers who are now his good friends. Although being aggressive in that way was not in my nature, I knew he was right, so I committed to give his idea a try. As I left for the concert, I grabbed a cassette tape containing rough mixes from my almost completed *Windows to the World* album. I stuffed the tape, a piece of notebook paper, and a pen in my pocket and headed out the door.

> *Many do with opportunities as children do at*
> *the seashore; they fill their little hands with sand,*
> *and then let the grains fall through,*
> *one by one, till all are gone.*
> —*Thomas Jones*

Although the concert was great, I couldn't fully enjoy it. I was in torment the whole time knowing that I had to be bold and create my own opportunity; there could be no procrastinating. The time was now! During the show I scribbled a few words on that piece of notebook paper and stuffed it into the cassette box. As the concert was coming to an end, they broke into "Roundabout," which they had been using as an encore number for years. That was my cue. I headed down to the floor level and tried to talk my way backstage. The fact that I'm a concert performer and somewhat experienced in getting around at these kinds of events usually gives me an edge. But no matter who I talked to or what I said, I could not convince security to give me passage backstage.

Frustrated, I finally gave my tape to the front-of-house sound man who promised to give it to Jon. As I handed it to him, I thought that was it. I can't get backstage, and now my tape is gone, probably headed for the trash can. By now they were playing their third encore, and I knew that my window of opportunity was closing. In one final attempt, I exited the coliseum into the freezing February night and circled around to the back of the arena. Over in an area where the equipment trucks unloaded, a policeman was sitting just inside a glass door. I knocked on the window and he cracked the door to see what I wanted. Yes was just hitting their last chord for the night.

At that instant, I caught sight of Jon about 50 yards away as he was being ushered down a ramp from the stage by two men. When it comes to seizing opportunities like this I've always been shy, almost introverted. But at this moment my instincts took over. I yelled out "Jon!" loudly enough to be heard over the still-roaring crowd inside. He looked over my way, and I caught his eye. He motioned for me to be let in, at which point one man walked over and said that Jon would see me once he had showered and freshened up a bit.

About 45 minutes later my musical mentor emerged, wearing a black full-length winter coat pieced together with overlapping scraps of cast off coats. There I was, face-to-face with my life-long musical hero. I was completely tongue-tied (which is unusual). To add to the tension, there were others standing around as well, causing me to be even more inhibited than I already was.

After a forgetful bit of small talk I said, "I'm a jazz guitar player, and I'm almost finished with my newest album. I gave a rough copy to your soundman. If he gives it to you, and if you like my music, would you ever consider working with me?"

Well, now I had done it! I had put him on the spot, and he didn't seem to know what to say. So he didn't say anything. Then someone else started talking to him, and I just stood there feeling about six inches tall. After a while I blurted out the same message again. "Jon, if you *really* like my music, would you consider working with me?"

He just looked at me, sighed, and said, "Well, anything is possible."

If you could look up the phrase "awkward moment" in the dictionary, this would have been the example given. What did I expect him to say? He didn't know me from Adam, and although I wanted to say so much, nothing was coming out right. So I said goodbye and headed home.

The next day I left for a one-week tour of colleges in the upper Midwest and Great Lakes areas. As the miles passed by one by one, I reflected back on my encounter with Jon, thinking, "Boy, I really blew it, and that's probably the last time I'll ever see him." But as you've probably surmised by now, that's not the end of this story; in fact, it's just the beginning.

A week later I returned home and headed over to my answering machine to check messages. There it was... my very first message. I could hardly believe it! It was Jon's distinctive voice, British accent and all, telling me that he not only liked my music, but also thought that maybe we could work on some songs together. ***Wow! I mean Woooooooow!*** For me there was no bigger thrill.

*If Elvis Presley, John Lennon, and Jimi Hendrix
had all reappeared one last time
just to sing on my record,
it wouldn't have compared to this.*

I played that message over and over. After scraping myself off the ceiling, it hit me what an incredible lesson I had learned. ***No one can predict the outcome when a person takes a chance and ventures forth in pursuit of a dream, but you can precisely predict what will happen if you don't... nothing.***

As excited as I was, I knew that pursuing this relationship further would not be easy. He had left the number of their management firm in Los Angeles, and I had to go through a maze of calls, explanations, and messages just to talk with him a second time. That was eleven years ago, and cultivating a relationship with a man who is almost always traveling took a lot of patience and persistence. But it eventually paid off. At one point, he invited me to Los Angeles where we rehearsed together for a possible Jon Anderson solo tour of China. There I was, playing "Owner of a Lonely Heart" with Jon's crystal clear voice singing out over the speakers, and I remember thinking, "It doesn't get any better than this!"

Since then, Jon and I have not only worked together writing songs, but we have developed a strong friendship as well. In fact, we wrote a song together called "ZuZu's Petals," which is on my next album.

> *Learn to listen.*
> *Opportunity could be knocking*
> *at your door very softly.*
>
> —*Frank Tyger*

My story doesn't end there. Recently, Yes played in Nashville at the Starwood Amphitheater in front of about ten thousand loyal fans. This time I went to the concert as a guest of Jon's to work out details for an album we're planning to record together. As we were chatting backstage, the crew was busy loading up the huge stage set into a row of long tractor-trailers with almost military precision. I couldn't help but think back to that summer concert where I had first seen him perform over twenty years ago and be amazed at how our paths had finally crossed. That night the army of trucks, buses, and crew members headed off for Atlanta to begin setting up the next day's show, but the following morning before leaving town Jon Anderson, Steve Howe (guitarist), Igor Khoroshev (keyboardist), and several crew members who had stayed behind dropped by my home for a visit and to check out my studio complex.

We had a wonderful time listening to music and conversing over an outdoor barbecue. But they were not here strictly for pleasure. Jon recorded for a short time, putting a few final touches on an upcoming VH1 special. All too soon it was time for them to catch a plane to Atlanta to catch up with the rest of the crew for that night's show.

That was in August. Four months later my lifelong dream of making a record with Jon Anderson came to pass when he and his wife Jane flew into Nashville, where we spent six weeks writing and recording together. In the first week we wrote and sketched out ideas for thirty songs! For the month that followed we arranged and recorded what we had written. Now things had come full circle. My daily routine was recording with Jon, and that, coupled with his extraordinary talent, has made this project nothing short of a dream come true. Besides immersing ourselves in music, we spent hours in conversation over good food and drink, sharing stories and developing a great friendship. One of my favorite memories is warming ourselves by the huge bonfires we would build at night after a day of recording. I can think of no better way to enjoy the passage of time than this.

When our time was up, I drove Jon and Jane to the airport, where they were headed for Canada to resume work on the next Yes album. I was thinking about how much I would miss them. Jon and Jane had become part of our family. As I am putting the final touches on this book, I am also daily continuing my work on this album, finishing up my guitar parts and adding some other musicians to complete the sound of each song. Every time we roll tape, and I hear Jon's voice and my guitar together, I am reminded of how wonderful things have turned out simply because I took the risk of making a fool of myself to meet him. *I jumped... and my net appeared.*

What a valuable lesson I have learned. As opportunities arise, this experience has given me courage to look people in the eye and introduce myself. You never know where it might lead. One thing is for certain, if I don't take the chance, I know exactly what will happen... nothing.

When is the last time you sensed an opportunity was nearby, but you didn't have the courage to seize the moment? Maybe you saw the head of your company in a restaurant, and you wanted to approach him or her and share your ideas, but you were afraid. Maybe you were sitting near someone interesting on an airplane but didn't have the courage to initiate a conversation. Perhaps you really hit it off with someone but didn't ask him or her for a date. Or maybe you had the chance to mend a relationship, but you held back. Remember: nothing ventured, nothing gained. Don't let your life be a series of missed opportunities. And if you are ever wondering whether you should take a chance and seize the moment, my answer is undeniably and unquestionably—

YES!

5

MY BIG HOLLYWOOD ADVENTURE

Welcome to the Hotel California...
You can check out any time you want
But you can never leave...

"Hotel California"
lyrics by Henley/Frey/Felder
(Eagles)

An LA State of Mind

Some people will tell you life is a test, that we are all here to learn lessons that will help strengthen our character and help us mature and evolve. There's certainly a lot of truth in that statement, but little did I know that Hollywood would prove to be my ultimate testing ground.

It seems that life always offers us a continuous stream of lessons to be learned. I have yet to meet anyone who is exempt from this universal truth. No matter what race, no matter what background, and regardless of how rich or how smart one is, everyone experiences challenges and adversities from the cradle to the grave. It's always seemed obvious to me that the extent to which we learn to master our emotions and learn to respond to adversity successfully will be in direct proportion to our personal and professional success in life.

As one who has been known to be just a touch stubborn—well, okay, *really* stubborn—I have often had to learn lesson after lesson the hardest possible way. Just when I thought I had learned them all, some new devastating challenge would arise, and instead of being at the front of the line ready to receive my "school of hard knocks" diploma, I'd be at the back of the line again.

> *I will tell you that there have been*
> *no failures in my life.*
> *I don't want to sound like some*
> *metaphysical queen,*
> *but there have been no failures.*
> *There have been some tremendous lessons.*
> *—Oprah Winfrey*

Moving to California always conjured up images of excitement, adventure, and opportunity. It almost seemed like a quest straight out of the Bible. I was on a mission to find a new life, and California was the Promised Land. In fact, heading west in pursuit of a more prosperous life... well, that's as American as apple pie! In the days of yesteryear, it was gold fever that brought people to California. In the '80s, when personal computers came on the scene, Silicon Valley became the land of opportunity for software designers who made millions.

Then there's show business. Come on... haven't you ever imagined yourself up on the silver screen? America has had a love affair and a fascination with Hollywood since the days of silent movies. For better or for worse, we have been raised in a nation greatly influenced by television, and we've all been transported into another world through movies that have inspired us.

Making my way through Los Angeles was like trying to navigate a ship without a map. I wasn't sure exactly where I was headed, but I was determined to get there. My persistence, sheer will power, and enthusiasm helped me overcome many obstacles and make my way through treacherous waters. I eventually stumbled and tumbled into some of the right doors. It's amazing how far you can go fueled by dreams.

The power of holding onto the hope of a dream
should never be taken for granted.
If a person has enough faith, enough desire,
enough determination and persistence,
he can accomplish almost anything.

My main problem was that at twenty-two years of age I was convinced I knew everything. The truth is, I was flying blind from the first day I landed on the West Coast, but I wasn't afraid to keep swinging until I got a hit or two. In spite of all this, I was actually well suited to the LA mentality and made myself right at home very quickly. Like any big city, LA was home to people leading dark and strange lives who should be avoided. But I made the best of it, and found that most people were actually pretty nice.

There's No Business Like Show Business

For seven years I earned my degree in street survival, pounding the pavement of Hollywood in pursuit of the almighty recording contract. The first thing I figured out was that there were thousands of others like myself arriving daily to break in to the music business. At first, this really took the wind out of my sails, but eventually I figured out that everyone else was as clueless as I was. When you come to LA it doesn't matter what you've done in the past. Everybody starts over from the same place—the bottom. This was especially hard for me because I had been making a living as a guitar player since I was eighteen. There were several misconceptions I had during this time of my life:

♦ *Mistake No. 1:* **Denial**— *"As long as I stay busy, I must be making good progress."*

♦ *Mistake No. 2:* **Pride**—*"I'm a professional musician, and I know what I'm doing."*

♦ *Mistake No. 3:* **Insecurity**—*"I'm not about to get a day job; then I won't be respected."*

♦ *Mistake No. 4:* **Fear**—*"I'm not going to just walk up to record executives, introduce myself, and hand them a tape. What if they don't like it?"*

> ***Sure I was climbing the ladder of success, but it was leaning against the wrong wall!***

Unfortunately, I spent almost five years of my time in Hollywood trying to accomplish the wrong goals. I was working hard, but I wasn't working smart. Every time someone said no, I took it as personal rejection. My confidence was low. I didn't understand how to seek out people who might have good advice, people who could mentor me. The truth was, I wasn't asking the right questions, and if someone did offer good advice, I had too much pride to really listen.

Back then I had never heard of
"personal development"
or the "science of personal achievement."
If someone had tried to
tell me about personal growth,
I probably would have thought they were trying
to recruit me for a religious cult.

What I *did* have was:
- A burning desire to succeed,
- Big dreams,
- A willingness to work hard,
- A willingness to really sacrifice,
- A boatload of determination and persistence.

When you get in a tight place and
everything goes against you,
till it seems as though you could not
hold on a minute longer,
never give up then, for that is just the time
and place the tide will turn.
—*Harriet Beecher Stowe*

Hollywood Castle

A walk down Sunset Boulevard in Hollywood was a surreal experience. Any time, day or night, you could find street performers, beggars, hookers, and religious fanatics handing out their pamphlets. It was the most unusual assortment of people you could ever imagine... a melting pot of renegades, rejects, and the elite from all four corners of the globe offering up every distraction and temptation imaginable. The streets were filled with limousines and exotic cars. The billboards spotlighted rock stars advertising the release of new albums or action scenes from current movies. Every secretary was an aspiring actress about to be discovered; every waiter had a movie script in progress. And everyone else—well, they were all trying to break into the music business.

As soon as I hit town, I spotted a rental ad in the paper. A few hours later I was signing a lease for a one-bedroom apartment in a grand old Spanish building called Malaga Castle, about two blocks from Hollywood and Vine. It was built in the 1930s by Paramount Pictures as housing for the young actresses who were signed to the studio in those days. In one section of the four-story structure there was a massive apartment suite which had been built for Gloria Swanson. It was right out of the movies, a true slice of Hollywood. Of the tenants in the building's (which *really* did look like a castle), thirty-five units at least twenty-five were trying to break into either the movie industry or the music business. Although I was broke and living hand to mouth, it was fun to be totally immersed in music. Every wannabe musician, scriptwriter, producer, director, and actor from the other forty-nine states was there with dreams of grandeur. Everyone I talked to was as obsessed as I was, and there was really only one subject anyone ever talked about... SHOW BUSINESS!

Robin's Big Hell's Angels Adventure

Everything I owned was in my truck—that's what I had to show for all the touring I had done so far. It was full of music gear and a complete concert sound and light system. I put an ad in the paper right away announcing "Sound and Lights for Rent." Almost immediately the phone started ringing, and I was in business. So off I'd go in my 1964 ex-U-Haul truck, and, two or three days a week, find myself hanging out backstage at some concert event—usually heavy metal or punk—babysitting my equipment and people-watching. For several years this was the way I paid the rent, so the rest of the time I could work on my music. Renting out my equipment gave me a taste of the music scene in Los Angeles. My education in street smarts accelerated when I began renting my gear to a promoter who put on all-day rock festivals in Thousand Oaks, just outside LA. Once a month, two to three thousand people would show up to see groups like Canned Heat and Steppenwolf headline after a day of local band wars. One Sunday the Hell's Angels, yes, the real Hell's Angels motorcycle gang, showed up—about fifty of them. It turns out they had a score to settle with some performer. They walked right on to the stage and a hush fell over the crowd. At first, there was a little pushing and yelling, but soon it erupted into a full scale brawl. That's when the security guards stepped in and all hell broke loose. It was terrifying. One guy had his head rammed into a nearby tree as some other gentleman picked up a microphone stand (yes, it was mine) and hit a stagehand hard enough to bend the shape of the stand—cartoon-style. Then another fight broke out over by the concession stand... people crashing through tables like a barroom brawl in a John Wayne western. There I was, with all my equipment, right in the middle of a barbaric display of male testosterone. It was frightening to know that my sound equipment could be destroyed at any moment. It didn't take long for an army of California State Troopers to show up. They broke out their shotguns and immediately gained the respect of the motorcycle gang. They lined up the Hell's Angels against a wall and shoved shotguns against their temples. It was right out of the movies. I thought to myself, "So this is how the West was won."

Sleepless in LA

Night and day I wrote songs. Eventually I got pretty good at it. To get studio time, I traded amplifiers and guitars, or I offered to do construction work—whatever it took. This is where I began my education as a recording artist... I cranked out demo tape after demo tape, pouring my heart and soul into every melody and lyric. I would scout around town handing them out to a few people that I assumed might be in a position to help. But if the criticism was too strong, I would retreat to my apartment like a wounded dog and it was *back to the drawing board*.

Once again, I would start writing and recording a new set of songs. The whole process would begin again.

Have you ever heard someone say that for every no you get, you are one step closer to a yes? Well, it's true. Before long, I found people who thought I had promise. A young production company funded my first real album. When it was finally finished two years later, I titled it *Legend of a Fool*. Looking back, that title couldn't have been more perfect. You'd have to be a serious collector to have one of these. Nevertheless, it was a great experience. I've always believed you can't create a great album until you make a few not-so-great ones.

An Entrepreneur Is Born

Those who seldom make mistakes
seldom make discoveries.
—*Sir John M. Templeton*

Life was never dull as long as I kept my ad in the paper to rent out my sound and light system. Every week I would find myself in some unusual or surreal concert situation as "New Wave" and "Punk" took over the music scene. Normally I would drive to the gig, set up my gear, and sit through the show. I always stayed right with my equipment to insure it wasn't abused or stolen. Once, I got a call from a band who wanted to rent my gear. They wanted to pick it up themselves so that they could save some money. It was for a nightclub called Mavericks Flat, a hip rhythm-and-blues and funk dance club. About ten guys came to my apartment and introduced themselves to me. They told me their club was located in Watts, which is just about the funkiest part of LA imaginable. Nonetheless they seemed like good people, and I trusted them. So I agreed and they loaded up the gear into a half dozen pickup trucks and vans and headed off. About a week later I was scheduled to meet them at the club at around two in the morning to retrieve my gear and get paid. Mavericks Flat turned out to be a night spot with style and class. It was very clean and well-kept, and everyone was well-dressed. Even at that late hour, there were people everywhere, including a few bouncers who could have been linebackers for the Miami Dolphins.

Out of a crowded room emerged a good-looking man who was tall and built like a brick wall. He introduced himself and asked me if I'd like to talk to him a minute in his upstairs office. About a half dozen men followed us up the stairs, and it quickly became clear that he was the man in charge. He got right to the point. The first words out of his mouth were, "Your speaker system sounds pretty good. I want you to build me one."

> I replied, "It would cost a lot. You have no idea."
> He asked, "How much?"
> I said, "At least fifteen thousand dollars."
> He replied, "Okay, build me one."

I didn't really take him seriously so I said, "Well, I'd need five thousand dollars down." He said he'd call me in a few days. I thought he was just a lot of hot air. A few weeks later, however, I did hear from him, so I returned to their offices where I was handed five thousand dollars cold cash. He didn't haggle with me… he didn't even ask me to sign for it. He simply trusted that I would deliver my promise.

To make a long story short, I pieced together a very professional sound system by calling all over LA and tracking down used equipment from concert sound systems. They were delighted with the results. At this point, I was told about a small building behind the club and asked if I knew how to turn it into a recording studio. Although I had absolutely no experience building record-ing studios, I believed I could do it. This was another time that I jumped, expecting the net to appear. Because they trusted me, I worked all the harder to pull the whole thing off successfully. I surrounded myself with people who knew how to build studios from the ground up, and slowly it all came together. It took the better part of a year to complete my mission, and when the studio was done they just loved it. Besides getting paid to build it, they let me record there as often as I wanted. Then they asked me to build them a huge video studio and sound-stage in yet another building. I never did get around to it because by then I was too busy with my band, playing dates around LA and pursuing a recording contract.

My experiences as an entrepreneur were invaluable. I had become very resourceful in a town that once scared me. But nothing that happened in my first six years there compared to the experience I was about to have with my new-found job as a limousine driver.

Most people tend to fear the unknown. Perhaps it boils down to how we adjust the way we view life:

- **As an adventure—or as a hardship**
- **Filled with opportunities—or disappointments**
- **Challenges—or problems**
- **Faith—or doubt**
- **Courage—or fear**

Creative Positive Expectation!

Now if we could just teach people that.
If the schools in this country
would teach children to look for the best and
believe they could accomplish the best,
they would be the best, and
we would have the greatest country
in the history of mankind.

—*Dr. Norman Vincent Peale*

6

CLOSE ENCOUNTERS

Driving Miss Daisy

After ten years of making my living either as a musician or an entrepreneur, I now had a real job as a limousine driver in Los Angeles. Many who knew me said I'd never be able to work for anybody else because I had become so independent over the years. This was my chance to determind whether I could work for others and submit to their authority. Driving a limousine seemed like it might be fun, but it was a cultural shock to find myself working for a company with structure, rules, and a dress code. It was the first time I had worked as an employee since my days of having summer jobs in high school. I had to go out and buy a three-piece suit and dress shoes and be on call four days a week.

I was twenty-eight years old, and little did I know that this job was going to provide me with more education in the music industry than the rest of my tenure in LA combined. In fact, that's when my Hollywood adventure really kicked in. All of a sudden, I was driving some of the biggest stars in the world and even getting to know them personally. I was hanging out at lavish Hollywood parties and getting paid for it!

But that's not how it started out. When you first begin driving for a limo service, you receive all the unimportant after-hours assignments. At 3:00 a.m. I'd get a call. "Can you be at the airport in one hour?" The airport was an hour away, so I'd jump out of bed, throw on my suit, and scramble to make it on time. On any given day it was not uncommon to drive for sixteen hours, go home, fall into bed, and an hour later receive a call from the dispatcher asking me again to be at the airport in an hour! I took everything they threw at me, and in just a couple of months I became a first-call driver. Just the fact that I was always ready to work impressed them enough to start giving me better assignments for bigger clients.

It was great! I drove Christopher Reeve, Mike Wallace, Pat Benatar, Mike Douglas, Melissa Manchester, Dolly Parton, Richard Pryor, Carol Burnett, Rod Stewart, and countless others—even Benji the dog!

Most of them were polite and gracious. One time Pat Benatar invited me in to have tea. Christopher Reeve and I talked up a storm one afternoon as I drove him home from a television interview. Melissa Manchester invited me to a birthday party she was having. It seemed the more successful they were, the more accessible they were. Perhaps they had stopped keeping score on how successful someone had to be in order to engage in conversation with them.

I learned a valuable lesson through my experience as a limo driver.

   I learned if a person is willing to:
      ♦ *commit*
        ♦ *go the extra mile*

♦ work hard
♦ be responsible
...he will stand out from the crowd.

When I moved to Hollywood I observed successful and famous people only from a distance. Then I went to work for them, first as a stagehand or a sound engineer, and later as a limousine driver. Then, as a musician and performer, I toured with these same people and opened up for their concerts.

Now, as a recording artist, I collaborate with them on my records, and as a studio owner I welcome them to my farm to record their music.

Fifteen years later, I am working with some of the same people for whom I once drove. More than once I've had the pleasure of reminiscing with them about the days when I used to be their chauffeur in Los Angeles.

Hello, Dolly

The success of Dolly Parton is one of the great American success stories of how dreams come true for those who have a spirit of determination, persistence, and a great attitude. Dolly's enormous success exemplifies this. I have witnessed her journey firsthand, having crossed paths three times over a twenty-year period.

When I first hit LA, I worked a couple of months in a big rehearsal facility where rock acts such as Led Zeppelin and Fleetwood Mac rehearsed before leaving on tour. Early one morning I arrived to find a tour bus with a butterfly painted on the back parked outside the loading dock. It belonged to Dolly Parton. I was sent over to escort her to the rehearsal stage. The thing that stood out to me was how incredibly polite she was. It was obvious she had been riding all night, but that didn't seem to dampen her pleasant attitude. She didn't have to smile, be polite, or even acknowledge my existence, but she did all of those things. I never forgot that.

Six years later I had taken a job as a limo driver, and I drove her to the Beverly Hills Hotel after an appearance on *The Mike Douglas Show* promoting her new movie, *Nine To Five*. By this time she had become a true superstar in every sense of the word. She was an international celebrity. As she headed from the television studio to the limousine, an army of people followed her. She was on top of the world, but was still gracious and courteous to everyone she came in contact with—including me.

A few years ago things once again had come full circle. One morning I remember my son Joseph asking me, "Who's in the studio today?", and I answered, "Dolly Parton." Wow! Dreams really do come true. It would have been hard to imagine this twenty years ago... Dolly Parton coming to my home and studio to work on her album. I believe dreaming big dreams has made the difference between success and failure in my own life. Now things like this happen almost daily.

Grant Me Honesty

Another example of someone whose attitude goes hand in hand with her success is Amy Grant. Hands down, I've never met anyone with a more sincere and pleasant personality. But what stands out to me is her honesty. Whether I'm talking to her one-on-one, or listening to her music, that transparency and honesty shines through.

Remarkably, she pioneered a genre of music when

she was just fifteen years old. She has paved the way for hundreds of other artists because of the barriers she has broken through, crossing over from contemporary Christian music to pop. One of the reasons she crosses boundaries is that people are naturally attracted to someone who is willing to lay her heart on the line and who is transparent. I can tell you that her genuine interest in the people she is around is at the heart of who she is.

Amy recorded many of her vocals and instrumental overdubs for her *Behind the Eyes* album at my farm. She worked on this album for two years, writing songs that dug deep below the surface—putting herself through a process of self-examination. Her inner voice shines through in each song. On that album, instead of writing formula hits, she wrote songs that were meaningful to her and from her heart. Amy has reminded me how important it is to be honest with myself and with those I have the privilege to touch.

Solitary Man

The six weeks Neil Diamond spent at Dark Horse while he recorded his *Tennessee Moon* album was the opportunity of a lifetime to hang around one of the most successful entertainers in the world. Nashville is known for having some of the finest songwriters anywhere, so it was no surprise that Neil had come to the Music City to write with the best. I had heard through the grapevine that he had been recording in some of the big studios on Music Row, the heart of Nashville's music industry. It seemed logical to me that he would only record in the most expensive and elite studios that Nashville had to offer.

Needless to say, I was thrilled to get a call from his

project coordinator asking if Neil's producer Bob Gaudio could come take a look at my studio. On a beautiful Saturday in May, he and a couple of production assistants came out for a visit. After checking things out, they seemed to think it would suit Neil just fine. He was now at the point in production with his album where the vocals were ready to be added to the already recorded music. This was only the second year since I had built my first studio—which we now call "The Cabin"—and long before I had expanded to a three-studio complex. Our private "make yourself at home" atmosphere was just what they were looking for. So we struck an agreement, and a month later there was Neil Diamond hanging out on *my* studio porch with his dog Sal, enjoying laid-back conversations and good cigars.

I was now immersed in the world of Neil Diamond. It was an amazing experience. After all, he has influenced pop music for all time with his incredible songwriting and vocal performances. He has written dozens of pop classics such as "Kentucky Woman," "Solitary Man," "Song Sung Blue," "Cracklin' Rose," "Sweet Caroline," "Love on the Rocks," and "America." I can't imagine any musician or songwriter who couldn't help but be influenced by his work. He has sold over 110 million albums and has set box office records at major venues all over the world.

The depth of his success and the scope of his work are inspiring and nothing less than awesome. Although he has enjoyed a relatively high profile in the music world this past decade, many people are totally unaware of some of the things he has done inside and outside of music. For example, Neil not only starred in the remake of the movie *The Jazz Singer*, but he also composed and performed the film's multi-platinum soundtrack album.

His duet ballad with Barbara Streisand, "You Don't Bring Me Flowers," reached #1 on the singles charts.

Looking at his track record, the list of his achievements is so long it's simply overwhelming, and he continues to come up with fresh ideas. In 1972, he performed a record-breaking twenty performances of a one-man show at the Winter Garden Theater, becoming the first rock-era superstar to headline on Broadway. He's done Christmas specials, HBO specials, and, in support of *Tennessee Moon*, he staged a television special from Nashville, part of which was filmed right here on our farm and then released as a home video.

In 1998, he released another video documenting his record-breaking double tour "Love In The Round," performed on a circular stage specially constructed in each arena. It's easy to see the constant creativity and innovative ideas that have kept him on top.

During his summer at Dark Horse, Neil was always focused like a bullet in flight. He would arrive every day around noon and would stay till about midnight, six days a week. When he wasn't in front of the microphone singing, he was kicking back in one of our rocking chairs reviewing his next song, going over lyrics and making last minute changes, right up to the moment he was laying it down on tape. Most albums have ten, or maybe twelve, songs at the most. But for Neil, that's just the beginning. To insure that every song on that album was a masterpiece, he wrote and recorded twenty-six songs to completion. This is truly an example of going the extra mile.

Neil Diamond has shown me a living example of how focus and commitment to excellence can really pay off. It's obvious that he loves what he does and has a tremendous passion for his music. I've seen other recording artists who breeze in for a week or two to lay down their vocals, and the rest of the time aren't even around for the recording of their records. But that certainly was not the case with Neil Diamond. During the recording of *Tennessee Moon* he could have been hanging out on a sunny beach at some lavish tropical resort, but instead he stayed totally involved with every aspect of the making of his album. That kind of passion translates into his continued success. You can't have thirty years of consistent sell-out concerts and hit records without it.

Why do I think you should know this about a man like Neil Diamond? I began to realize that he was possibly the most passionate, focused, and hard-working person I have ever known. And guess what? He's also the most successful. Do you think there just might be a correlation between the two? Absolutely! Neil is living proof that success is no accident. That's not to take anything away from his extraordinary voice or his prolific songwriting. His talent is unquestionable, but the fact that his career has stood the test of time is a testament to his skill as a man who understands the laws of success.

Needless to say, I have gained an incredible appreciation for Neil Diamond the man and Neil Diamond the artist. I have seen firsthand a living example of success in action and have been inspired to higher levels for my own work. The last night he was here we celebrated with an outdoor barbecue. Everyone was in high spirits. His daughter had flown in to visit for the last few days, and that afternoon she had mentioned to me how much she would enjoy going for a horse ride. As everyone was finishing their meal, I came racing up on my favorite horse, Blackfoot (surely by now you must have figured out that a studio called Dark Horse Recording has horses!), and asked Neil if he would mind if I took his daughter for a ride.

He said, "Absolutely not!"
I replied, "Oh, but I have insurance."
Neil asked, "How much do you have?"
I smiled and said, "A half million dollars'
   worth."
"That wouldn't cover her big toe!"
   he answered with a sly grin.

That helped put things right into perspective. My life has been enriched because of crossing paths with this solitary man. Thank you, Neil.

7

BEATING
THE ODDS

Every failure brings with it the seed
for an equal or greater opportunity.
—*Napoleon Hill*

The holy grail of the music business is a record deal with a major label such as Warner Brothers, Sony, MCA, Virgin, Arista, etc. It's what every singer/songwriter lives for and works toward. Bands in every town and city in America dream of getting a big recording contract and then watching their songs rocket up the *Billboard* charts. They hope to film music videos destined for the top ten on MTV or VH1. They believe that if somehow they could magically land that elusive recording contract, big concert tours and all the other trappings of success would be sure to follow. For countless aspiring singers and musicians, this is the American dream.

After years of bad advice, half-cocked dreams,
Shooting in the dark with hare-brained schemes,
I broke the doors that stood in my way,
And landed a deal with RCA!

Walking down the Avenue of the Americas in New York City on the way to my first meeting as a signed artist with RCA's new imprint label, Rendezvous Entertainment, gave me a feeling of sheer ecstasy. It was incredible! In every direction there were thousands of people scurrying about. There must have been a hundred musicians on every block who had come to this city with the dream of landing a major record deal as well. I thought to myself, "How did I get here? Why me? What did I do to deserve this? Was it because I had more talent?"

Of course not. I have always known scores of musicians who have more natural talent than I do. Was it luck? No way! I had been preparing for this moment since my teens. I had spent years playing in every imaginable situation: sleazy clubs, county fairs, high school assemblies, and eventually hundreds of college and university campuses. I had spent years living a gypsy-like existence on the road and latter struggling to survive in Los Angeles. Even after moving to Nashville in search of sanity and a more balanced lifestyle, I was out of town most of the time—living a dream on one hand and sacrificing everything in the name of music on the other.

Have you ever heard the joke about the man who sees his friend sweeping the floor backstage at a rundown theater and says, "Buddy, you need to get out of here and find yourself a better job." His friend replies, "What? And give up show business?"

Please don't let me give you the wrong impression. Things were going along pretty well. Life was good. I had five national albums under my belt on smaller labels and was making a good living as a concert performer. Each album I recorded was better than the one before as I became more skilled at my craft. But I dreamed of taking things to a higher level and proving to myself that I could measure up. Finally, I determined to land a deal with a major label no matter what it took.

It's truly amazing—
The obstacles you can overcome—
When you set your sights higher
With determination, faith, and desire.

If I had known the odds for pulling this off were about the same as winning the state lottery—or getting struck by lightning on the way to buy a winning lottery ticket!—I might not have set my sights on a career as a recording artist. But music has always been my passion. So year after year I followed my heart, traveling thousands of miles to give concerts and spending hundreds of studio hours behind the microphone making records. My recordings never sold in big numbers, but I did have a small, loyal following. The turning point came when I made a conscious decision to become a major label artist, *or bust.* I discovered that as soon as a person truly commits to a goal, the *way* to achieve that goal will reveal itself.

Betting Everything on One Song

Now that I had albums out, I thought the days of having to record demo tapes were over. But I knew that in order to land a major record deal, I needed new music on tape that was more powerful than anything I had done before. So, with the help of some of the finest musicians in Nashville, and after several hundred hours in the studio, I finally completed a demo tape that I was thrilled with. If not for the great musicians and engineers getting behind my cause, I would never have been able to create such a great sounding tape. After spending six months laboring over these new songs, I knew there was no turning back. At last I was ready to lay it on the line. In the past I would play my demo tapes for a few people, then quickly retreat upon receiving too much negative criticism. I realized the biggest trap keeping me from the success of landing a major record contract was fear—I was paralyzed by fear.

> ♦ *Fear of rejection.*
>> ♦ *Fear of failure.*
>>> ♦ *Fear of success.*
>>>> ♦ *Fear of pain.*
>>>>> ♦ *Fear of the unknown.*

I decided that the only way I could deal with my fear was to face it, *to look at it eye to eye and take action in spite of it.*

My new manager, Ken Mansfield (who had previously worked for the Beatles, managing Apple Records), laid out a strategy which began with sending out about 35 letters to record label executives, to be followed by a one-song cassette tape upon request. The letter announced that he was so positive he had a winner that listening to one song was all it would take. This bold, forceful approach landed us about a dozen requests for a tape.

Unfortunately, the overall response to the tape was thumbs down.

Next we mailed out about fifty three-song cassette tapes and once again...

No positive response.

My first inclination was to call it quits because all this rejection was so painful. But Ken really believed in my music and assured me that many other artists who had gone on to have great success had endured the same kind of rejection. We gave it one more try. We compiled a list of 137 record company executives and sent each one of them a package, including a revised tape of these songs, and at last...

We got a couple of bites!

The first bite was from Arista, but after a while we could tell the excitement was wearing off and most likely nothing was going to come of it. Then, on a Saturday afternoon, Ken received a call from Jimmy Ienner, a major player in the music business. The timing was perfect. He was heading up a new label called Rendezvous, under the RCA umbrella, and was signing a few new artists. His career successes read like a "who's who" in the music industry. Groups like Pink Floyd, Blood, Sweat & Tears, Three Dog Night, Grand Funk Railroad, and KISS were just a few of the acts that he helped steer to great success. He had a passion for my music and caught my vision of incorporating that music into live multi-media events. Although it was avant-garde, he considered that a positive. He had seen how this had worked for Pink Floyd, and believed the time was right to put the weight of his record company behind me. Almost immediately he put me in the studio, and six months later *Electric Cinema* hit the streets. Overnight, my new record was in over 10,000 stores and was being played on radio stations across the country. Instantly, new opportunities opened up. I had the privilege of appearing on national television many times and was invited to perform in bigger and more prestigious concert settings than I ever had before.

Having a record on a major label in the stores gave me the added credibility I needed to get a loan for my farm. Many other doors were opened to me that helped to establish a more solid foundation under my career. All those new opportunities more than offset the rejection and pain that I endured along the way. It was wonderful!

You might say I just got lucky... but I don't think so. Remember, one of the most important principles of success is persistence. Consider Thomas Edison, who experienced over ten thousand failures before perfecting the incandescent light bulb, or Walt Disney, who was turned down by 403 banks while trying to raise money to create Disney Land. Think about it. Perhaps if Ken and I had sent out only 136 tapes, we would not have landed the deal. Through persistence we beat the odds. Once you understand this, success will no longer seem like some mysterious or magical event that is available only to others. Every person I know who has accomplished great things has possessed drive, determination, and persistence as their greatest weapons. This has certainly proved true in my case. Getting signed to Rendezvous/RCA was one of the most challenging experiences of my life, and although *Electric Cinema* never sold a million copies or had a smash hit on the radio, it was a success with the critics. Most importantly, landing this record deal gave me self-confidence and taught me valuable lessons about holding onto a dream. It instilled the belief that anything is possible. That belief is more valuable to me than any record deal or financial reward.

> **Success comes to those who become**
> **success conscious.**
>
> —*Napoleon Hill*

No matter how overwhelming your quest may be, never give up. Most people who are great successes have had more failures than failures do, but the difference is they persevere and never quit. In my office I have a notebook containing *over 80 letters of rejection* that preceded the **long-awaited "Yes"** from RCA! From time to time, I'll look through that notebook as a source of encouragement. It's a reminder of how I beat the odds.

I have included a few of these rejection letters on the following pages. If you are facing what seems to be insurmountable odds, perhaps these letters will inspire and motivate you to keep on keeping on!

Chrysalis Music Group

Chrysalis Music (ASCAP)
Chrysalis Songs (BMI)
9255 Sunset Boulevard, Suite 319
Los Angeles, California 90069-3498
Telephone: 310-550-0171

Fax: 310-281-8750

810 7th Avenue
New York, NY 10019
Telephone: 212-603-8769
Fax: 212-603-8759

Chrysalis

8 April 1992

Mr. Ken Mansfield
Front Row Management
2005 Convent Place
Nashville, Tennessee 37212

Dear Ken:

I'm sorry to have taken so long to respond to the Robin
Crowe material. The sale, the move, new employees, etc.
have kept me tied up with minutia rather than music.

At any rate, I've listened through a couple of times and
asked my staff to do the same. Regretfully, we cannot
muster enough enthusiasm, from a musical standpoint, to
propell a deal through.

Please keep me informed on your other projects however,
and I'll look forward to seeing you when you're next in
Los Angeles.

Yours sincerely,

Tom Sturges
Senior Vice President and GM

TPS:dmr

EMI
810 Seventh Avenue
New York, New York 10019

MICHAEL BARACKMAN
Vice President, A & R

September 26, 1990

Ken Mansfield
MAIN MANSFIELD ASSOCIATES
United Artists Tower
50 Music Square, Suite 200
Nashville, Tennessee 37203

Ken:

Oh boy. I noticed that I never had responded to you regarding Robin
Crow. This one totally fell through the cracks. I apologize profusely.
It is embarrassing that you had sent me this so long ago without me
responding. There is no excuse.

For what it's worth, I did go through the package. I heard it more
for a New Age type of label a la Private Music. It wasn't really
something we could have sunk our teeth into. I did enjoy it (and would
enjoy a CD if you have an extra one). Perhaps there is something more
mainstream-slanted that we can work together on.

I respect what you do, and would enjoy working together. I'll try to
hold up my end of the bargain in the future.

BEst,

Michael Barackman

MB/gl

Tel 212 603 8618
Fax 212 603 8681/2

MAIN MANSFIELD
A S S O C I A T E S

May 15, 1991

Ken
Good energy, but
I don't hear a breakthrough
hit single which might
launch the artist.
I'll have to pass.
RS

Arista Records
Richard Sweret
Six West 57th Street
New York, NY   10019

Dear Richard:

A few months ago you expressed interest (after hearing
a one song tape I sent you) on Robin Crow.

So........here's five more new "monster" recordings which
he has just completed.

Robin has been tearing up the college circuit with his
intense stage show; and has developed quite a large following
over the last few years. Let me know what you think---there
are more songs, press info., video, etc., if interested.

Warmest regards,

Ken Mansfield
President

KM/clc

Enclosure

P.O. BOX 50146   NASHVILLE, TN 37205   (615)665-2250   FAX (615)665-2340

Ken Mansfield
Main Mansfield Assocs.
P.O. Box 50146
Nashville, TN37205

June 21st 1991

Dear Ken,

Thankyou for sending me the <u>Robin Crow</u> tape to listen to which we have just been doing thismorning.

Getting straight to the point, I am really not a great fan of 'muso.' types of project - by which I mean where technique and musical ability are the main attraction. Robin's playing (and the production here) is very impressive, but it all sounds a bit serious and bombastic for these ears. I really believe attitude and great ideas are of paramount importance, over and above how musically proficient an artist is. Also, this is really not the type of artist Imago is looking to get involved with and develop.

Thus, I have to say that this is a pass. Robin seems to be the sort of artist that Wyndham Hill or Elektra/Nonesuch might appreciate a little more than I.

Thanks again, and good luck!

Sincerely,

Hugo Burnham
Director, A&R

The Imago Recording Company
152 West 57th Street
New York, New York 10019
TEL (212) 246·6644·FAX (212) 246·0404

EPIC
RECORDS

CBS Records Inc.
1801 Century Park West
Los Angeles, California 90067-6406
(213) 556-4700

March 27, 1990

Mr. Ken Mansfield
Main Mansfield Associates
50 Music Square West, #200
Nashville, TN 37203

RE: ROBIN CROW

Dear Ken,

I've had a chance to review the enclosed materials
on Robin's music. It all sounds great and he's
an excellent guitar player but I don't feel that
Epic is the appropriate place for him. He belongs
on a label that can cater more closely to him and
his type of music. Labels that might be appropriate
for him include GRP, Restless and Guitar World's
new label.

I appreciate you keeping Epic in mind for Robin and
wish you luck in finding a home for him.

Regards,

Ken Komisar
Senior Director
West Coast A&R

KK:dac

enc.

April 10, 1990

Dick Whitehouse
CURB RECORDS
3907 W. Alameda Avenue
7th Floor
Burbank, CA   91505

Dear Dick:

A quick hello!!

ROBIN CROW ??

Let me know!!

Warmest regards,   4.23   Should I say "Let's Go!" ?

                                    I wish it were so because
                                    I think Mr. Crow spells "dough" --
Ken Mansfield   but only for those in the
President   know ... (ie not in country type)

KM/cg   Sugar, Private Music, Navada,
                                    Notus, or Windam Hill --
                                    Michael Hedges notwithstanding.

                                    Ken, This guy's great

ATLANTIC

RECORDING

CORPORATION

9229

SUNSET

BLVD.

LOS ANGELES,

CA 90069

TELEPHONE:

(213) 205-7450

FAX:

(213) 205-7475

April 21, 1991

Ken Mansfield
Main Mansfield Associates
P.O. Box 50146
Nashville, TN 37205

Dear Ken:

Thank you for submitting material to us. I found the tape
interesting, however, instrumental tracks are unfortunately
not what I am looking for at this moment. He did have an
ear-catching sound, though.

Please feel free to send any additional material that you may
have in the future.

Best Regards,

Kevin Williamson

KW:tob

ARISTA RECORDS, INC.
Arista Building
6 West 57th Street
New York, NY 10019
(212) 830-2252

MITCHELL COHEN
VICE PRESIDENT
A & R, EAST COAST

March 26, 1990

Ken Mansfield
Main Mansfield Associates
United Artists Tower
50 Music Square West
Suite 200
Nashville, TN 37203

Dear Ken:

I reviewed the video cassette you sent by Robin Crow, and although
he is a talented and creative guitarist, I really don't feel that
his compositions or performances show breakthrough potential.
Since I don't hear the kind of distinctive musical qualities that
would make a real impact, I'm going to pass on this porject, but
I appreciate your bringing Robin to Arista's attention.

Yours truly,

Mitchell Cohen

MAIN MANSFIELD
A S S O C I A T E S

November 9, 1990

David Stamm
ARISTA RECORDS
Six West 57th Street
New York, NY   10019

Dear David:

Per your request I submit a more in-depth look at ROBIN CROW.
You asked for original material, so I have enclosed Robin's two
most recent CDs which include mainly his compositions.

The one song cassette of "The Wall" that sparked your interest in
Robin is more in the musical direction he would like to pursue at
this time.

Thanks for your interest. Enjoy, and I look forward to your response.

Warmest regards,

Ken Mansfield
President

KM/cg

Enclosures

P.S. I have a video -- just ask!!

12-13

Ken -
He's a talented performer,
but the compositions and
overall concept don't strike me
as particularly compelling or unique.
So I'll have to pass on the
project for now. I do, however,
appreciate your sending the
material along.

David

PolyGram Records™

* *

May 16, 1990

Ken Mansfield
United Artists Tower
50 Music Square West, #200
Nashville, TN 37203

Dear Ken:

Sorry it's taken me so long to respond to Robin Crow, but I
finally got a chance to view his video. I was very impressed with
his guitar technique, but I feel he would be better served on a
label that specializes in New Age/Progressive rock type artists.
For this reason I am going to take a pass.

Again, I am sorry it's taken me so long to get back to you, and
if you come across any other exciting artists send them along.

Best wishes,

Tom Vickers

Tom Vickers
Director A&R
PolyGram/Wing Records

PolyGram Records, Inc.   Telephone: (818) 955-5200   Casablanca
3800 West Alameda Avenue   Fax: (818) 848-7530   Mercury
Suite 1500   Telex: 9104902149   Polydor
Burbank, CA 91505   PolyGram Classics
                                                                    Wing

8

ROBIN'S RATHER LARGE TREEHOUSE

Impossibility: a word only to be found
in the dictionary of fools.

—*Napoleon Bonaparte*

This is the story of how I began building wealth. Most importantly, this is the story of how I broke though my own self-conceived limitations and discovered new levels of potential that I didn't know existed. This is the story of how, on a leap of faith, with $2,000 and a couple of sketches in hand, I embarked on an enormous project that was to become my own enchanted castle! This castle took shape in the form of an 8,000-square-foot world-class recording facility constructed of hundreds of huge timbers, complete with horse stables, a fifty-foot lookout tower, multi-level lounges, guestrooms, and a state-of-the-art kitchen that looks up into a thirty-foot steeple! From the inside you feel as though you're in a giant treehouse right out of a storybook fantasy. When it was all said and done, my dream that started with $2,000 appraised for almost *one and a half million dollars!* Before I tell you how I pulled this off, please allow me to back up a bit.

Over $100,000 a year and always broke?

Over time I had built a wonderful career. My albums were in stores nationwide, and every year I would perform a hundred concerts or so, earning over six figures annually. I kept asking myself...

Why was I almost always operating in the red?
Why was I still living hand-to-mouth?
Where did all the money go?

Spending in the entertainment industry is like jumping into an abyss—*it's endless!* For starters, I had a full-time staff who coordinated my concert tours and a road crew in charge of maintaining the six thousand pounds of sound and lighting equipment my crew and I hauled around the country. I was constantly upgrading gear in an effort to keep up with the latest technology. I had an enormous phone and postage bill each month due to outrageous promotional expenses, music industry conventions I attended, and so on. There was an endless assortment of managers, agents, accountants, lawyers, promoters, publicists, and investors to be paid as well. Did I mention graphic artists, photographers, stage and lighting designers, and huge transportation expenses? There was simply never enough.

In spite of my financial black hole, I managed to scrape together enough money to make a down payment on a small farm in Franklin, Tennessee, a few miles outside of Nashville. On it was a large log house constructed from four different cabins from the 1830s. It was a bit drafty but had lots of atmosphere. At last, my wife, Nancy, and I had a great place for raising our children. After twenty years of touring and waking up in a different city every day it was time for a change, and this was my chance to stay home with my family and concentrate on recording. Immediately I began construction on a small but very professional studio attached to the back corner of our new home. The idea was to have a place to work on my own music and to produce other projects as well.

There's a joke around town…

Question:
How do you a make a million dollars
in the studio business?
Answer: You spend two million on a studio!

Everyone told me I was making a huge mistake. But I followed my heart and built the kind of studio that I had always wanted to record in. Once it was up and running, I called a few friends who produced and suggested that they might enjoy renting the studio from time to time when I wasn't working on my own projects. I thought this would help offset expenses.

Dark Horse Recording seemed like the perfect name for my studio because the dark horse is the unexpected winner in a horse race—the long shot. What made my studio stand out from others was the private and earthy atmosphere. The whole place was filled with plants, skylights, and windows overlooking the countryside. Musicians could come here and count on not only high quality equipment and sound, but also a unique nature-based environment.

Within a year and a half word of mouth had spread, and people like Neil Diamond and Faith Hill were cutting platinum albums here. I had stumbled into the studio business!

Question: Do you know how to make God laugh?
Answer: Just tell Him your plans!

This all came about at a time when I was becoming disillusioned with the music industry. Every year it seemed to be less about art and more about commerce. I was no longer with RCA and unsure in which direction to proceed. My studio was booked for a couple of months ahead so I had some time to think about things and some steady income as well.

I knew it was time for a change so I took a step back to put things in perspective.

It was then that I had a moment of revealing clarity...

- *How can I unlock my true potential?*
- *How can I break through the fears that have been holding me back?*
- *How can I raise my life to a new and higher standard?*
- *What if I fixed my mind on a goal so big, I won't have any time to open myself up to negative influences?*

These questions left me with a desire and a vision to create and achieve something unequivocal.
I wanted to build something that reflected the triumph of the human spirit!
By taking action on that vision my life has been completely changed.

During this time I began plans to build a simple horse barn. My new vision began to manifest itself in the project. It seemed like a wonderful idea to combine a studio and horse stables in the same building. So I took out some notebook paper and began jotting ideas down. I had absolutely no idea how I could raise the money, nor did I have a clue how much it would cost to complete it. If I could just get the basic structure up, I figured I'd work the rest out as I went along.

With Only $2,000 I Began

My first step was to hire a bulldozer to clear out a building site and reshape the hillside. At this point the building was not much more than ideas and a sketch on paper. It was to be 115 feet long, 65 feet wide, and just over 50 feet tall at the highest point. I was already out of money when the bulldozer was finished. But the process had begun, and I now had a spot to stand on, to touch and feel, to visualize and determine how to take things to the next step. Initially, Willie Anderson (my neighbor, who just happens to be an excellent barn builder) helped me bring the structure into existence. With the help of his two-man crew we began pouring footers and erecting the first level.

The scope of the project was so huge relative to my limited financial resources that in the beginning I didn't even tell my friends what I was up to.

One thing was for sure. This was going to be a great opportunity to further my education in:

♦ *Staying focused.*
  ♦ *Cultivating a positive attitude.*
    ♦ *Harnessing the power of follow-through.*
      ♦ *Dealing with adversity.*

Now my horse stable/studio building was underway. My plan was to build it with huge timbers and windows throughout, every view creating the effect that you were looking out from an enormous treehouse. By this time Pioneer Log Systems, the timber framing company, was piecing hundreds of huge timbers into place like an enormous puzzle. It looked like an Amish barn-raising, except that there was a crane effortlessly hoisting the giant beams into place.

> **Opportunity is missed by most people**
> **because it is dressed in overalls**
> **and looks like work.**
> — *Thomas Edison*

As the project grew, new possibilities came to light. With the help of Stan Justice and Bobby York (two master craftsmen), I added a fifty-foot lookout tower and a spectacular kitchen with a cathedral ceiling looking up into a thirty-foot steeple. In fact, I credit Stan with taking my ideas and turning them into reality. As the project progressed, I suggested changes almost daily, and it began to take on a life of its own. No matter how impractical or outrageous my ideas were, Stan would always come up with a way to pull them off. I've had other projects where carpenters would moan and groan every time my suggestions were a bit too creative or pushed against their comfort zone. There is much to be said for holding on to that childlike spirit of looking at the world as a place full of wondrous possibilities.

As the design evolved, the floor plan became a maze of interesting twists and turns. There wasn't a square room or hallway in the entire building. It even had a spiral staircase made from hand-notched wooden beams! I kept adding windows of different sizes until we had installed 142 of them! Then we built decks all around, looking out over the countryside. About that time I met Ted Judy, an artist in wood, and an accomplished singer-songwriter as well. In the beginning, Ted was going to help trim out windows in a couple of rooms... he is still hammering away! Never have I met a person more gifted or who takes more pride in his work, and it really shines through in the incredible custom cabinetry and trim details throughout the building. Ted has become a member of the Dark Horse family as he continues to add a seemingly endless array of final touches on all four floors, even though we have long since been up and running. The building is like a huge painting taking on its own character as it matures. I often think to myself: *Let this be an expression of art. After all, isn't art a reflection of the personality behind the creation?*

As I got opinions from various contractors, I couldn't believe how inconsistent and conflicting they were, so it always came down to taking my best shot and *making a decision*! When standing at the crossroads, I always ask myself, "What do I have to lose?" The answer is always the same: "Not that much!"

In hindsight, there are many aspects of the project I would do differently, but what was most important for me was the act of following through and finishing this massive building.

During the first year of construction I put my musical projects on hold and worked on the building all my waking hours, often by myself. As I worked, I listened to tapes by personal development speakers such as Napoleon Hill, Brian Tracy, and Tony Robbins for countless hours on end. The more I listened and learned, the stronger my confidence grew. For the first time in my life I began to understand that I was capable of achieving dreams that I once thought impossible. In fact, if not for the powerful coaching I received from these great thinkers, I don't think I would have had the courage to go face to face with the banking world, which ultimately lead to my million-dollar-plus loan. The constant encouragement I received while listening to these tapes was invaluable. They helped fuel my spirit with the seemingly inexhaustible supply of determination, desire, and will power it took to see this project through.

> *What the mind of man can conceive and believe,*
> *the mind of man can achieve.*
> —*Napoleon Hill*

It's exciting to plant a seed of thought and watch it grow. In this case, what started out as a simple idea for a horse barn had taken on a life of its own. It was an enormous undertaking, unlike anything I had ever imagined. **Jump... and the net will appear** became my mantra. My attitude was "W*hat's the point of being alive if you miss out on all the possibilities for passion and adventure?*"

Jumping

I've always believed that the way to accomplish overwhelming feats is to have faith, take courage, and then jump in and begin. Planning and organizing in great detail before starting a project is good common sense, but I have seen instances where over-planning can be a recipe for crippling procrastination. This is not to take anything away from my admiration for someone with a well-thought out and comprehensive business plan. It's amazing what can be accomplished when you plan your course of action, but you must make the commitment to follow through. Otherwise, planning can become refusal to jump. The commitment to follow-through produces leverage that will drive you forward one step at a time.

It's like preparing to drive cross-country from Los Angeles to Atlanta. It's only natural to mentally break the trip down into smaller steps. As someone who has traveled extensively, I can vouch for this. The thought of driving 2,191 miles at once is too daunting a task. Instead, visualize taking a break after 272 miles, which would land you in Las Vegas, perhaps taking time to catch a show or to try your luck at the tables for a few hours. Now, rejuvenated, move on to Flagstaff, and then perhaps Albuquerque, and so on, until, before you know it, you're on the home stretch to Atlanta. There's no way I could have ever completed this new studio without breaking it down into a thousand small steps, each obtainable one by one.

The dreamers are the saviors of the world.
Composer, sculptor, painter,
poet, prophet, sage,
these are the makers of the afterworld,
the architects of heaven.
The world is beautiful because they lived;
without them, laboring humanity would perish.
—James Allen

Risky Business

Any time you take a great risk, you stand the chance of losing big. The higher the risk, the greater the loss can be. When you reach for a star it's a long way to fall, and as a husband and father of four, I am acutely aware of this. But I have a supportive wife and family who trust that no matter what happens, we will have each other and, one way or another, we will survive and be happy.

How Did I Get the Money?

By now you may be wondering where I got the money to complete this rather large treehouse. Good question!

It's amazing how creative you can be when you lay it all on the line. My family sacrificed in every area of our lives. We cut expenses to the bone. We took on the mindset that having a big goal would be a thrilling adventure, that it would be exciting to work on it together and imagine it finished. We sold one of our cars, leaving one car for a family of six, but as it turned out, the reward of not having two vehicles outweighed the inconveniences. We took no vacations, would rarely go out to eat, and committed to a low consumption attitude toward clothes and furniture. There is much to be said for a simple and focused lifestyle. None of these sacrifices brought unhappiness or stress to our household. In fact, they gave us a sense of unity, mission, and love.

But that only got us a fraction of the way there. By the time I had invested approximately $30,000 in this project, my only immediate resource left was to start running up my credit cards. I would have never used the cards for personal luxuries, but this building was to be a workplace. I believed with all my heart the second studio would pay back the entire investment as my first one had, so I was willing to take some chances. This was not for the weak of heart. *I ran up $85,000 on the cards in three months!*

> **A man cannot directly choose his circumstances,**
> **but he can choose his thoughts, and so indirectly,**
> **yet surely, shape his circumstances.**
> —*James Allen*

My next step was to secure financing. Surely any banker would see what a great plan I had and sign me up for a big loan. Wrong... I was turned down by two dozen banks... it was humiliating. But after three months of people telling me it couldn't be done... I did it! I found a company that was willing to paint outside the lines. Their plan was to secure an initial loan borrowing against the value of my property. After several appraisals I discovered that, after four years of continual improve-ments, the value of my property had quadrupled! Great news! That's what the bank wanted to hear. The money came through... breathing new life into the project. The loan money was like fuel to keep moving things along. But this initial loan provided only enough funds to bring the building to about 75% completion. It was like climbing a huge mountain and now I could see the top. I was three-quarters of the way there, and I was more determined than ever to keep going and somehow find a way to reach the peak.

It was nerve-wracking, but once again running up my credit cards was the only way I could keep things moving toward final completion. This time I ran them up to $134,000!!!!! I carefully renewed all of them to get the low introductory rates. Now my highest interest rate was 6.9%, which is better than a bank loan but, of course, you know how it works: after six months the interest shoots back up to 19% or 20%. This is how the credit card companies lure people in and then go for the kill. I was on a race against time.

Once again I was on the hunt for a loan. I was betting that with the increased value of the new studio, I would be able to borrow enough money to pay the credit cards back down, all $134,000. The risk was great. There was the distinct possibility that I could put my family in financial ruin.

There I was, back on the streets in search of a lender who was also a believer in my mission. After countless rejections I managed to find someone willing to take a chance on me.

My final loan was for over one million dollars!
Not bad for a self-employed musician...
once and for all I had proved to myself
that any dream is possible and
any goal is achievable if you back it up
with faith, determination, and persistence.

It was another six months before I finished the building to the point where we could begin installing all the studio equipment. Four months after that we were ready to make music. It had been three years and three months from the day I brought in that bulldozer to the day we fired up the studio and began recording. Never had I done anything so challenging, but the finished results were well worth it.

With a Little Help from My Friends

There is no such thing as a self-made man.
You will reach your goals
only with the help of others.

—George Shinn

Make no mistake. I could not have gotten this project off the ground without help from my family and friends. I had set out to build something extraordinary, and my enthusiasm attracted helping hands from some unlikely places. More than once my parents bailed me out when I painted myself into a financial corner. For instance, about one year into the construction it was winter and seemed to be raining every other day. The entire framework of the building was up and the roof was ready to be shingled. Only about half of the outside walls and windows were in, and whenever a rain storm hit, the building took a real beating. My folks came to the rescue. Many times over the years they've lent me money, but this time they presented me with a gift—enough to help me get the building dried in.

My neighbors would come over to help lift beams into place and my friends and family helped on weekends to paint or clean up the job sight. In fact, my father drove up from Texas several times and helped me paint the interior. My two teenaged boys, Andrew and Joseph, put in hundreds of hours assisting me, and I know the memory of what we accomplished together will be a lifelong reminder of their capabilities. There is no doubt we will continue to add onto and improve this building for years to come. It will always be a work in progress.

One of life's greatest pleasures is working together with others on a worthy goal.

Thoughts are powerful. Every extraordinary thing that mankind has ever done began as a little seed in someone's mind. Sending a man to the moon started as a simple idea, but before long we had done it—A MAN ON THE MOON! We live in a society in which people can get crushed by a system that doesn't necessarily support individuality or creativity. We are taught from day one to conform and to be normal, yet many of the people who have accomplished extraordinary things were misfits. Somehow they persevered. For me, building this *rather large treehouse* has been a metaphor for living life.

If You Build It, They Will Come

Since the day we turned on the recording equipment in the new studio, which we call "The Lodge," the phone has been ringing with people requesting recording time. The very first month we were open my studio income tripled! Six months later we are still steaming ahead at full capacity, and I have learned a valuable lesson from this. By putting in all that extra effort and going the extra mile in every area of this project, the rewards have been tenfold. All that extra effort has paid off exponentially.

The Long Run

On any large project it's easy to go through periods of wanting to throw in the towel and settling for less than we hope to achieve. But remember: the race always goes to those who endure in the long run. True victory is about perseverance, determination, and never giving up. When I was in the middle of this project, I was exhausted from working on it sometimes 100 hours a week, and I was tired of being turned down by so many banks. To make matters worse, the studio business had taken a downward turn because of sagging sales in the country music industry and, at the same time, a dozen new studios were being built in the Franklin area alone. But I was already in motion, and I knew that if I didn't get the money, successfully finish the studio, and overcome all those obstacles, it would mean bankruptcy for me and my family. That was powerful leverage for finding a way to succeed. Every day I found a reason to keep on going, and when it was complete I had something I could really be proud of.

Remember that the benefits of accomplishing a worthy goal always go deeper than just making a profit or checking off another achievement. It will give you confidence and strength of character, which will give you wings to take flight with your dreams and to far exceed your self-imposed limitations. Now is the time to stop operating out of fear and to take control of your destiny. It is time to tap into your almost infinite potential waiting to be discovered.

Take heart and know that
you possess the power to realize
your highest aspirations and dreams.

9

PUSHING THE ENVELOPE

Two years ago I took my two sons to see the movie *The Lost World: Jurassic Park,* and on the way home we were marveling at how, through Steven Spielberg's direction, those artists and technicians brought dinosaurs to life with computer imagery. If you've ever seen one of the dinosaur movies from the fifties, I think you'll agree that in just a short time we've progressed light years technologically from the days of black-and-white monster movies. Time after time, man has achieved extraordinary advances by pressing against his limited thinking and boundaries. Technological advances in the film industry are just one example. Man is constantly finding ways to push past limitations.

> *This little story makes a big point about overcoming limitations and expanding our circle of possibilities.*

In the early '90s, I was touring in a Ryder truck. It wasn't as plush as those $400,000 tour buses that most acts travel in, but, hey… it was paid for. The front section was converted into a camper, not unlike the old U-haul I had driven fifteen years earlier. It was, however, much nicer. I always took a two-man crew and they were in charge of setting up the 6,000 pounds of sound and lighting equipment we carried from city to city. Their jobs kept them busy around the clock. After driving hundreds of miles a day we would arrive at the concert site, and they would jump into action managing the unloading of all our lights and speakers, rear screen projectors, guitars, and other gear, and then taking care of the countless details leading up to show time. Once my performance was finished, they would reverse the whole process and begin packing the truck back up. As soon as the truck was loaded, we would dead-head toward tomorrow's destination, taking turns at the wheel while the others slept. It was not uncommon to repeat this four or five days in a row before slowing to catch our breath. It would be easy to look at this as a torturous lifestyle, but we loved it!

> *In order to have a rainbow,*
> *you have to put up with a little rain.*
> —*Dolly Parton*

There is something very romantic about traveling across America this way, experiencing firsthand all the richness this country has to offer. The life of a traveling musician is a funny thing. Once you've experienced that kind of freedom, you're hooked. From then on it's in your blood, and it tugs at your very soul. There's no turning back.

Expanding Our Beliefs

It was the middle of February, and we were touring up north. We were just wrapping up a ten-day run, playing our last concert at the University of Minnesota in Morris. My office received a last minute call from Maryville College in St. Louis asking if we could perform the day following the Minnesota concert. The catch was that the concert had to start at noon.

Under normal circumstances, the drive from Morris, Minnesota, to St. Louis, Missouri would not have been possible. Not only was it a 700-mile trek, but there were no direct highways even remotely connecting these two cities. We would have less than 11 hours to get there. But a crew member observed that we would be passing through St. Louis on our way home anyway, and it was simply a matter of arriving a few hours earlier. After a short debate we decided that we should give it a try and think of it as an adventure.

Sometimes a person doesn't know what
his capabilities really are
until he steps out on faith and jumps.
If you don't jump you will
never know what you can achieve in life.

Although common sense was not on our side, the lure of everyone earning an extra day's pay was leverage enough. With map in hand, we began to plot out a complex route, cutting back and forth on county roads and two-lane state highways. We figured if we averaged 70 miles per hour, there was a chance we could arrive in St. Louis by 11:00 a.m., leaving us an hour to unload the truck and set up all our gear. By the way, our average speed, figuring stops, was usually only 45 miles per hour. It was amazing to see all the time-saving solutions we discovered.

First, we called a meeting with our local stage crew (furnished by the University of Minnesota) and explained that we had to come up with a plan to load up the truck in just 30 minutes instead of the usual one and one-half hours it normally took. Everyone was up for the challenge, so we assigned each person a detailed list of tasks to accomplish at the show's end. As the stage set went up that afternoon, my crew carefully explained to each stagehand how every piece of equipment would be packed up and loaded later that evening. My crew and I had always thought we were organized, but now we had raised the bar to a new level. As my concert came to a close, everyone sprang into action, and with military precision my crew and ten stage hands successfully tore down, packed, and loaded 6,000 pounds of gear in just over 30 minutes. We were on our way.

We turned every gas refill into a pit stop. One person would pump gas, one would check under the hood, and another person would pay. Besides having a designated driver, we also had a designated navigator and we continuously debated all our routing options as we made our way across country. We challenged ourselves to not waste a single minute. We were so excited by our mission that none of us slept a wink all night.

Guess what? That night we drove over seven hundred miles in eleven hours without sleep, and, under the worst road conditions imaginable, we showed up at Maryville College fifteen minutes before show time! With the help of a couple of dozen students who muscled my gear onto the stage, we pulled off that afternoon concert without a hitch. Within a few hours we were headed on home to Nashville, ahead of the original schedule that was set up before the St. Louis stop came into play. We were ecstatic! The fact that we earned extra money was negligible compared to the lesson we learned about overcoming our perceived limitations.

By pushing the envelope of our touring abilities, driving five to six hundred miles a day between shows became a breeze. Think of athletes in training. That's exactly how they stretch their limitations; they continually push themselves to the next plateau. What was once an overwhelming feat becomes commonplace, just as a runner might constantly push himself to higher levels. We can all do the same in every area of our lives. As we raise our standards of excellence in our relationships, in our health, in our faith, and in our careers, we are shaping our destiny. We will create an extraordinary quality of life.

> *The pessimist sees*
> *difficulty in every opportunity.*
> *The optimist sees*
> *opportunity in every difficulty.*
> —*Winston Churchill*

10

ARE WE HAVING FUN YET?

*If you're not experiencing happiness and
enjoying the passage of time
as you move through your daily life,
you've got to ask yourself,
"When will I begin?
What has to occur for me to be happy?"*

Are we having fun yet? Often I'll hear someone say that in jest when they're putting in a grueling day on the road or in the recording studio. But it's a good question. It refers to an ultimate paradox: the more a person seeks happiness through the quest of acquisitions and achievement, the more happiness will elude him. Financial success is wonderful, but you and I know it will never bring lasting happiness. What good is it if a man builds a castle on a hill and then lives in it by himself? We've all seen people who seem to have everything going for them, yet they're still not happy. This is often because of set expectations that have to occur, expectations that will never be met. Instead of focusing on all the beauty and abundance in their lives, they continue to focus on what's not perfect or on unmet expectations. In the music world there's a long list of talented people whose lives were cut short who fit into this category: Keith Moon of The Who... Jimi Hendrix... Kurt Cobain of Nirvana... Janis Joplin... John Bonham of Led Zeppelin... to name just a few. It seemed these people had absolutely everything they desired, yet they were miserable. They were willing to risk their own lives for the illusion of happiness. On the other hand, I know people who seem to have little or nothing in the way of finances or possessions, they have failing health, or they have to work long hours just to make ends meet, but they always wear smiles on their faces and have an attitude of thankfulness. As odd as it may seem, these people are the ones who have found happiness.

> *Remember, happiness doesn't depend*
> *upon who you are or what you have;*
> *it depends solely upon what you think.*
> —*Dale Carnegie*

<u>What do you think is going to bring you happiness?</u>
- ♦ *Winning the lottery?*
- ♦ *Admiration from others?*
- ♦ *Appreciation?*
- ♦ *Becoming the first millionaire on your block?*
- ♦ *Riding the perfect wave?*
- ♦ *Giving the perfect concert?*
- ♦ *Experiencing the perfect football game?*
- ♦ *The biggest house, the most impressive car?*
- ♦ *Trophy children?*
- ♦ *A spectacular achievement?*
- ♦ *A room full of awards?*
- ♦ *Will you be happy if you get a facelift or work out until you acquire the perfect physique?*

What will it take? Although some of these things might be worthy endeavors, when you think it through it becomes clear that none of these will ever bring the kind of lifelong happiness we desire: a rich, fulfilling satisfaction underlying good times and bad. Our culture teaches that we should continually raise our material standards for happiness as we progress through life. It's the big lie and we all know it, but we still get swept up in the mentality that material wealth equals happiness. It is natural to desire a happy and rewarding life. Unfortunately, too often we end up looking in all the wrong places for that happiness and fulfillment. If our goal in life is based on what we can get instead of what we can give, our lives will be empty and unfulfilled.

Looking back on the last twenty years of touring, I figure I have traveled well over a million miles on the highway. This has given me a lot of time to ponder the question of happiness. I've met people from every walk of life—rich and poor, young and old—and it is obvious that lasting happiness will never come from outside circumstances.

Lasting happiness will never come from:

- ◆ *Making money*   ◆ *Achieving power*
- ◆ *Giving a great concert* ◆ *Taking vacations*
- ◆ *Finding romance*   ◆ *Winning awards*
- ◆ *Becoming famous*

I could go on for days, but I'm sure you get the point. To find happiness in our outer world, we must first find happiness in our inner world. It is natural to seek happiness in our lives, but we must be careful that we are not seeking it outside ourselves. The more we chase happiness, the more it will elude us. Happiness is discovered as we spend our energy giving to others. It's actually very simple:

when people are active, when they feel the days have meaning, when they feel that what they are doing is beneficial to others, then they live in the zone of joy and happiness.

> *The only way to avoid being miserable*
> *is not to have enough leisure to*
> *wonder whether you are happy or not.*
> —*George Bernard Shaw*

Sometime happiness is disguised as sacrifice. Nancy and I now have three boys and a little girl... they are all depending on me to be a good provider and to offer up solid leadership. The continual responsibility is sometimes overwhelming, but it's the richest part of my life—the part that brings the deepest joy. As any parent would agree, the rewards that come from raising a family far outweigh any amount of sacrifice involved. By letting go of our self-centered desires in order to focus our energies on the needs of loved ones and family, we begin to discover the secret to happiness. Perhaps it can only be attained by giving it away. **Happiness and success will follow from the blessing we bring to others.**

> *Happiness is not a state to arrive at but,*
> *rather, a manner of traveling.*
> —*Samuel Johnson*

Are You Living in the Twilight Zone?

Years ago I saw an old black-and-white episode of *The*

Twilight Zone. This is the gist of the story. A man I'll call Grant died, and the next thing he knew he was in a fabulous penthouse suite surrounded by beautiful furniture, beautiful art, and beautiful women who waited on him hand and foot as they continuously admired him. He could play piano like a virtuoso concert performer, and everyone laughed at his jokes. He won every game of cards, and when he played pool he made absolutely every shot, no matter how difficult. As he looked at his new surroundings, his tailor-made clothes, his custom furniture, the priceless art hanging on the walls, he said, "This must be heaven."

Another man was present who was there to assist Grant and fulfill his every request. Grant often conversed with this man, telling him how much he was enjoying his newfound existence. At last he had the life he thought he had always wanted, where nothing could go wrong. Everything seemed perfect, yet something wasn't right and he couldn't quite put his finger on it. It didn't take long until the pleasure he had been getting out of his perfect life began to turn sour. He began to miss his old life where there was constant challenge and surprise. At last Grant said to his host, "Maybe this *heaven* is not for me. I'm bored with all this. Perhaps I should give the other side a try." The host looked him in the eye and said, "You're already there, my friend. **This is hell**." Wouldn't you agree that life *would* be a living hell if there were no adversities to overcome and no challenges to face?

What is Wealth?

It is impossible to give more than you receive.
—Mike Rayburn

Building lasting wealth is about focusing on what we can give instead of what we can get. Perhaps the best definition of abundance that I can give is to be both very successful in accumulating material wealth and at the same time maintaining a deep-rooted sense of spirituality. It is truly impossible to give more than you receive, and this principle is the essence of becoming successful at building material wealth. It is a spiritual law that applies to everyone without prejudice.

When one door of happiness closes, another opens;
but often we look so long at the closed door
that we do not see the one that has been opened for us.
—Helen Keller

A person's business life and spiritual life should go hand in hand. His spiritual life should be reflected in the way he runs his business, the way he treats fellow workers, and the way he treats his competitors. It goes without saying that honesty and integrity are fundamental ingredients for earning the respect of others. Happiness comes from spiritual abundance, not from material abundance. It's not hard to measure someone's material wealth, but in order to gauge spiritual wealth we must look at our lives. How do we value our life and the lives of others? Do we have meaningful, deep relationships? Are we using the gifts God has blessed us with for the good of others?

Happiness is like the air we breathe.
We can't see it, we can't buy or sell it, we can't horde it.
No one can put it in a box or behind glass...
It is, rather, a gift from God
to be experienced, to be savored, to be enjoyed!

11

ONLY THE SMART SURVIVE

Hard work is important.
Hard work is satisfying.
Hard work builds character.
Hard work alone is not enough!

Hard work is good for the soul... it builds character... it brings satisfaction... but in order to be successful you must also work smart! As I was growing up, my parents instilled a strong work ethic and for that I'll be forever grateful. When I was 14 years old, I began my own one-man lawn mowing service. I remember going door to door soliciting clients. In fact, I got about a dozen of my neighbors to hire me to mow their lawns for the summer. By the time I was 15, I had saved up enough money to buy a radial arm saw, and I began building speaker boxes. Pretty soon I was building them for my high school band (back then we called it a combo) and for other local bands as well. By the time I was twenty, I had learned to build complete sound systems. I had an old U-Haul truck filled with thousands of pounds of equipment, most of which I had built. You might be saying, "What an industrious young man,"... thank you... but here's the catch. I was spending way too much time building, thinking that somehow being well-equipped would lead me to success. In my own mind I would tell myself, "I'm working really hard here and therefore I *will* succeed." I was working but not learning... working but not practicing enough... using my brawn instead of my brain. My willingness to work hard became a double-edged sword. On one hand I had become a great survivor and learned a lot about woodworking and sound systems, but on the other hand I was not reaching my goal to be the best guitarist I could be and land a recording contract. Eventually I did straighten out my priorities and began a heavier concentration on my abilities as a musician and songwriter, but getting sidetracked with my "building habit" cost me years of precious time.

I remember the day that I began working smarter. It was a time of crisis. Because of some poor decisions, my career was in jeopardy. I was deep in debt... worn out... feeling very insecure... in fact, I was feeling like a total failure. I remember sitting by myself in the middle of a large field and realizing, "I am here because of making decisions without thinking things through. I am here because I didn't educate myself or ask advice from people who have been through these very same things." All of a sudden it was clear that I had to totally change the way I ran my life and career. **It was a defining moment in my life when I realized I needed to look before I leaped.** From that time on I began to work smarter and smarter. For me that meant changing old habits. It was the beginning of my new life. I became an investigator searching for clues to the answers to my questions. My new thinking changed everything. Whether

I was practicing guitar, trying to land a recording contract, or repairing my failing U-haul truck, I learned that by working smarter I could accomplish more than by simply working hard. Don't get me wrong. I still believe in hard work, and these days I've been putting in lots of long hours to prove it. I'm currently finishing up this book, putting final touches on my new album, overseeing Dark Horse Recording, and raising a family. Oh, yes—I'm putting time in every day finishing up the album I'm producing with Jon Anderson. I get more results for every hour of time I invest than ever before. There is a personal satisfaction that comes from a disciplined approach to work, but the person who *also* puts his knowledge to work is the one who succeeds!

> *If you want them to show you the money,*
> *you better show them the reason.*
> —*Harvey Mackay*

If you are always in the mode of accumulating knowledge, then knowledge becomes the tool that gives you the winner's edge. The most successful people I know have a childlike spirit of curiosity. They're not afraid to ask questions. They're not afraid to be inquisitive. According to the American Booksellers Association, 58% of Americans never read another book cover to cover once they leave high school. Can you believe that 70% of American adults have not visited a bookstore in the last five years? In fact, the average American reads less than one book per year. In a world where knowledge has become our most valuable resource, this is a sobering statistic. A famous pop star told me that the mark of a successful recording artist is someone who has made the largest number of wise decisions during his or her career.

Don't you think this applies to anyone in any walk of life? In this day and age it is survival of the smartest.

You might be saying, "Hey, didn't you say *Jump... and the Net Will Appear*?" That's right, but if you don't make sure that your *Jump* is backed by some careful research and planning, you could get into serious trouble. You don't want to leap off the high dive before making sure the water is deep enough to shield you from the jagged, rocky bottom. After you weigh all the variables, then you will have the fortitude to launch into a graceful swan dive with ease and confidence.

If this book were for skydivers, I might call it **Jump... and the Parachute Will Open**. Anyone who decides to try his hand at skydiving is a risk-taker, but he must go through a long, detailed checklist each time to best insure his safety. First, you make sure the parachute is packed correctly. If you're going to go barreling out of a plane at 12,000 feet, free-fall through the air, and then pull that ripcord with confidence, you must be well prepared. You must also have an understanding of wind currents and downdrafts. When skydiving, there is no room for error. There are no second chances. By the same token, when a "once in a lifetime" opportunity crosses your path, such as being asked for your own ideas during an interview for your dream job, it is crucial to be prepared. **Sooner or later wonderful opportunities *will* arise, and the secret is being prepared to meet them.**

Great Questions Lead to Great Decisions

One good decision can start you on the path that leads

straight to the fulfillment of your goals. On the other hand, one bad decision can steer you astray from the very thing you are hoping to achieve. What a wonderful thing it would be if we had the knowledge to correctly guide us through every decision we make. It is true that "knowledge is power."

There are two kinds of people: those who are on a never-ending quest for knowledge and are forever asking questions and those who are content to walk through life clueless.

Remember that there is no such thing as a stupid question. The more curious you are, the more you learn. The more you learn, the more successful you will become. **Let this become your success cycle.**

Most people are happy to share what they've learned through their experiences. It's human nature to want to pass on knowledge. So don't be afraid to ask. You'll be pleasantly surprised at people's willingness to stop what they're doing and impart their nuggets of wisdom when they see that you're eager to learn. What if you picked up one helpful gem of knowledge every day? In a year's time you would be exploding with great ideas, which would help propel you on to the achievement of your dreams.

As the owner of a recording studio, I'm constantly making new friends, people with whom I might never have crossed paths otherwise. We often sit around trading war stories about our adventures on the road or our dealings with record companies. I have gained a tremendous education listening to their experiences. Over the last several years, I have had the privilege of having some veteran record producers and record industry executives work here at Dark Horse. During coffee and lunch breaks, I'll ask their advice and attempt to learn from their experience. In some cases, I have made major decisions based on these conversations. **Sometimes small distinctions can change the course of our actions and become catalysts for powerful change in our lives.**

> *Most men believe that it would benefit them if*
> *they could get a little from those who have more.*
> *How much more would they benefit if they*
> *could learn from those who know more.*
>
> —*William J. H. Boetcker*

Quite often I will ask people what their career plans are. They tell me how it's all going to turn out for them, speaking with so much confidence they convince themselves and those around them that they *will* achieve greatness. As I listen I'm thinking, "They're making some big mistakes here. I remember when I used to think that way." I'll politely try to explain that I've been through what they're now experiencing, and I begin sharing a few ideas. Unfortunately, often they're not interested in what I, or anyone else, has to say. What a shame. Imagine what mankind could accomplish if everyone was constantly seeking knowledge and we were all sharing what we know. Our accomplishments would grow at an exponential rate!

Finding A Role Model

Imagine how much time you could save by benefiting from the experiences of others. Who do you know who has expertise in an area of interest to you? Seek out that person and emulate him. Find people whose personal and professional lives you admire and take note of their habits and values. People don't become successful by chance. This just might save you from some avoidable and unnecessary hard lessons.

What I'm saying is this—the more you learn and educate yourself, the more confidence you will have stacked in your favor when you do finally *jump*. This is not to take anything away from the childlike spirit of passion and excitement that inspires someone to get up early and stay up late in the pursuit of dreams. This is not to detract from that adventurous spirit that tells you to *jump* when others are not willing—or to *jump* when others are negative and discouraging about your desires and dreams. It's always about balancing out the two, because either extreme can prove harmful.

> *Man's only limitation, within reason,*
> *lies in the development and use of his imagination.*
> —*Napoleon Hill*

Questions... The Mother of Invention

We've all heard that "necessity is the mother of invention." That's why we are at our best when facing a crisis. When we're backed into a corner, our survival instincts come alive, and we come up with new and creative solutions we might never have considered otherwise. When we are overwhelmed with adversity, the human spirit seems to soar the highest.

As Tony Robbins has often said, the process of asking questions is at the root of how we learn and mature. If you want to change the quality of your life, you must change the kinds of questions you're asking. Your mind is always asking an endless list of questions. When you're in a moment of crisis it asks, "How can I get out of this?" When a football player walks on the field, he's asking questions: "How can I get the ball? How can I score a touchdown? How can I keep that 250-pound gorilla from doing a tap dance on my face?" The questions we ask determine the thoughts that fuel our actions.

If you want positive answers, ask positive questions. For instance, "How can I earn more and work fewer hours?" or, "How can I have a closer and richer relationship with my wife?" Your mind *will* come up with answers; it has no choice. That's simply the way our minds work.

On the other hand, if you ask, "How come life is so hard?" or "Why wasn't I born rich?" you will end up in a tailspin of self-pity and bitterness. The quality of your life is in direct proportion to the quality of the questions you ask. Don't underestimate the power of asking questions, because they will have a massive effect on the course of your life.

As I said before, it's no longer survival of the fittest, but instead it's survival of the smartest. All the successful people I have ever known are not only hard workers, but also in a constant state of curiosity—they have learned to work smart.

> *Arrogance is believing you're so high up that*
> *you don't have to keep an ear to the ground.*
> *—Harvey Mackay*

12

KILL THE BEAR

The growth of the human mind is still
high adventure, in many ways the
highest adventure on earth.

—*Norman Cousins*

Have you ever seen the movie *The Edge?* It's an action-thriller starring Anthony Hopkins and Alec Baldwin that spins a great story about the power of the mind. Hopkins plays an aging billionaire who is wise, insightful, and hyper-intellectual. The movie begins to unfold as he flies into the Alaskan wilderness in his $20 million jet with his supermodel wife and her high-fashion entourage for a photo shoot against the backdrop of the Great White North. Baldwin portrays a hedonistic and worldly fashion photographer who is deceitful and weak. An opening scene foreshadows the premise of the movie: that thinking smart enables one to overcome adversity.

Upon hearing that Hopkins' character has an uncanny ability to recall any piece of information he has ever read, the grizzled owner of the remote lodge puts Hopkins to the test. Hanging on the wall of the lodge is a boat oar with the image of a panther carved into the facing side. He tells Hopkins that he will give him five dollars if he can guess what's on the reverse side of that oar. Without hesitating, Hopkins answers, "It's a rabbit smoking a pipe." He was right!

"The rabbit is unafraid," he added, "because *he knows that he is smarter than the panther.*"

The next day Hopkins, Baldwin, and an assistant fly off in a smaller plane to an even more remote area in search of the perfect location for their shoot. Unfortunately, their outing takes a tragic turn when they intercept a flock of migrating birds. Their engine stalls, and in seconds the plane begins to spiral downward, resulting in a chilling crash landing in a mountain lake. Three of the four men on board manage to survive the crash, but are left stranded in the remote mountains to fight against nature. They have no food, no water, no life-sustaining provisions except for seven matches. But those problems become incidental, when, the next day, their real dilemma emerges: an angry, man-eating, 1,400-pound Kodiak bear picks up their scent and begins an aggressive assault. After a heart-pounding chase, they narrowly escape, crossing a deep river gorge on a fallen tree trunk. Later that night, in a surprise attack, the bear kills the assistant photographer and sends Hopkins and Baldwin running for their lives. Now the suspense really begins.

> ***To conquer fear is the beginning of wisdom.***
> —*Bertrand Russell*

It's a classic tale of two archetypes of male power thrown into extreme crisis—a crisis where they must fight insurmountable odds in order to survive.

"Do you know why most people die in the wilderness?" Hopkins asks. "They die of shame. They die because they didn't do the one thing that could have saved their lives—***thinking***."

There are several subplots woven throughout the story, but the one I find most interesting is the contrast between the personalities of these two men. With only a pocketknife and a few matches, they try to stay alive. The plot becomes a story of courage and inner strength. Their mettle is tested from the moment of impact. As they work together to survive, they are forced to forge an uncomfortable and restless bond.

Overcome by fear, Baldwin cries out, "The bear won't let us eat. He's always one step ahead of us. He's stalking us!" It's obvious that they are doomed to be hunted down by the killer bear. But the wise and composed Anthony Hopkins realizes there is another way... a way that takes a fearless and courageous life or death stand. ***They must turn and face the bear; in fact, they must kill the bear.*** He forces Baldwin to repeat over and over, "We're gonna kill the bear, we're gonna kill the bear." Hopkins yells, "*Say it again: We're going to kill the bear. Do you believe it?!*"

Over and over they yell, "We're going to kill the bear," until you are convinced they can do it. Hopkins knows that the only chance they have to kill the bear is if they really *believe* they can do it. It becomes a story that **celebrates not survival of the *fittest*, but survival of the *smartest*.**

The next morning the battle ensues, and Hopkins and Baldwin are ready. There is no possible way they can begin to match the brute strength of the bear, so it becomes a battle of wits. Within a circle of fire where they've built traps and made spears, they wage a formidable defense of their own. Both of them reach deep inside themselves, find that inner strength, and then they rise to the challenge. **In the end they triumph.** *They kill the bear.*

How do they do it? They outsmart him. They survive because Hopkins knows their only weapon is the power of their minds over the physical strength of the bear.

You know what? Once they slay the bear, several other problems are immediately solved. Besides freeing themselves from the life-threatening man-eater, they now have plenty of food—barbecued bear ribs—and a couple of fur coats. Most importantly, they gain a new level of confidence. They walk away feeling ten feet tall, knowing they could do it all again if they needed to. They now are thriving on their wilderness experience. What started out as a nightmare has turned around and become a personal victory for Hopkins and Baldwin.

> *What would you do?*
>   *Would you give up?*
>   *Would you run?*
>   *Would you give in to the strength of the bear?*
>   *Would you stand your ground and face him?*

Often, when we are faced with overwhelming odds, we reach down into the depths of our souls and find a God-given strength that we didn't even know existed. These are the times when we are at our best. We rise to the occasion, and we achieve something, that unequivocal and definite *something*. It is truly a triumph of the human spirit.

All of us have our own fears to face. For some it might be procrastination, perhaps something as simple as balancing your checkbook, or avoiding doing your taxes. Have you ever wanted to build your dream house, but the project seemed so overwhelming you were afraid to take that first step? Or maybe it's overcoming your fear of starting your own business or sitting down and writing that novel you've always dreamed about. Every time you dare to look fear in the face you gain strength, courage, and confidence. Are you haunted by fear—or by a *bear* in your life? This can be the moment of truth for you. *It's time to turn and face the bear!*

> **I've lived through this horror.**
> **I can take the next thing that comes along.**
> **You must do the thing you think you cannot do.**
> —*Eleanor Roosevelt*

The story in the movie *The Edge* is analogous to my own struggles in life. The week that I wrote this chapter, I closed on a loan for $1,040,000 to complete my new studio. I remember that only a few years ago I couldn't get arrested in a bank, unless I was to stage a hold-up. I couldn't get a loan of any size!

I was terrified at the thought of filling out all those applications. I made up banking jokes to compensate for my homespun accounting practices. I associated so much pain with the possibility of being rejected that I wouldn't even apply.

But...

About six years ago I was willing to go through anything in order to buy my first home. It took months of jumping through hoops, but I followed through and succeeded. That was like killing my first bear.

Remember, I was a self-employed musician. In the banking world, that's just one level up from an ex-con!

After I did it once, I knew I could do it again.

Now I can walk into a bank with confidence knowing that I can talk intelligently about finances. Now I can face them and ask for almost a million dollars and not be afraid. In fact, I can even get them to say yes!

—∞—

If you have the desire...
the desire to turn
and face the bear...
to stand up and proclaim
victory over him...
then you will kill the bear.

—∞—

13

NO LIMITS

Here are seven keys to realizing a life with no limits:

- ♦ Shape your destiny with a strong *vision*
- ♦ Understand the power of *beliefs*
- ♦ Acknowledge your unlimited *potential*
- ♦ Fuel your dreams with *passion*
- ♦ Discover God's gift of *abundance*
- ♦ Embrace *change*
- ♦ Learn the joy of *contribution.*

Do you want to see how high is high? It's my guess that you wouldn't be reading this book unless the answer was yes. So let's get started on a journey that will change your life. First, let's ask a few questions...

- ♦ Why do people let fear of the unknown become a crippling enemy that holds them back?
- ♦ Why do so many people settle for a life where they are just getting by... where expectations are low and so are the rewards?
- ♦ Why do some people stay in abusive relationships; or continually operate in a state of crisis?
- ♦ Why is it that so many give up the hope of achieving their dreams?

We all know that it can be painful to change old patterns of behavior such as poor diet or hours of television each day. For some it is more comfortable to remain in that state than to do what is necessary to change. But I promise if you give yourself good enough reasons, the ability to take the necessary steps will awaken within you.

There was a time when I had had all I could take and began to hit my threshold. I began to realize that if I didn't get clear on my goals in life, I would be destined to achieve the goals of others. Dissatisfaction with the way things are can be a good thing. It produces the leverage you need to bring about change. That's the way it was for me. I was tired of waking up every day of my life with the feeling that I was being controlled by outside circumstances. It was easy to give a thousand excuses for my situation, but the turning point came when I realized that it was up to no one but me to take responsibility for the way things were in my life. I knew there had to be a way to live with more passion, inner peace, and fulfillment—and I was determined to find it. I was finally committed to raise my standards and create an extraordinary quality of life. In fact, I was so thirsty for change that I began a quest for answers, studying personal growth and human potential. I read books and listened to audio learning tapes for hundreds of hours. It became my wonderful obsession.

Unlimited Vision

"Where there is no vision, the people perish . . ."
—Proverbs 29:18

Personal and professional success starts with having a great vision, because the next thing you know, everything you do begins to align with that vision. It's as if the cosmic tumblers of the universe begin to fall into place when you focus on that vision. With a strong vision, everything you do becomes a quest, and your search for that vision empowers you with a deeper sense of mission. That vision will compel you to do things you never thought possible. You will find yourself getting up early and staying up late, not because you have to... but because you want to.

> *If we want to discover the*
> *unlimited possibilities within us,*
> *we must find a goal big enough and*
> *grand enough to push beyond*
> *our limits and discover*
> *our true potential.*
>
> —*Anthony Robbins*

It's true that when you have a strong vision and make your goals a necessity, your mind starts looking for ways to overcome obstacles and break through barriers that might stand in your way. Before you know it, you will gain momentum that makes you virtually unstoppable. This might sound a bit mystical, but you will simply be following universal principals that will bring order into your life. Once you begin to take consistent action toward the fulfillment of your vision, you begin to unlock the secrets that lead to great achievement. All this will begin to pull you in a new direction... toward lifelong success and happiness. It all starts with the vision you hold in your head.

Beliefs

Sometimes it's better not to ask
—or to listen—
when people tell you something can't be done.
I didn't ask for permission or approval.
I just went ahead and did it.

—*Michael Dell*

When Michael Dell was eighteen, his parents had been alerted that he wasn't attending classes at his college and his grades were going down. In an effort to head this problem off at the pass they flew to Austin for a surprise visit. At that time, he was upgrading personal computers in his dorm room at the University of Texas. When he got the call from the airport saying they were in town and on their way, he barely had time to hide all the computers behind the shower curtain before they walked in.

When his dad began exhorting him about getting his priorities straight and concentrating on school, Michael's reply was, "**I want to compete with IBM.**" His father was not impressed. You've got to admit that that statement does sound preposterous coming from a teenager. But before his freshman year was up, he was selling between $50,000 and $80,000 per month in upgraded computers. Fifteen years later, Dell Computer Corporation is an $18 billion company, the second-largest manufacturer and marketer of computers in the world! Think about it. When he was eighteen years old his *belief* set his course in motion. It was his *belief* that enabled him to make that statement to his father. It was his *belief* that became a source of strength propelling him to beat insurmountable odds.

*It's hard to fight an enemy who has
outposts in your head.*

—*Sally Kempton*

You will never change your life until you change your beliefs about what you are capable of. So many people believe that their outer circumstances are controlling their lives. But it's our beliefs that shape our future. **What we believe fuels our passion and courage to go forth in the pursuit of our dreams.** We hear stories every day about people who overcame overwhelming adversities and went on to high levels of achievement. The force that drives them boils down to their beliefs in what is possible. Their beliefs make the difference. The reason that an optimist will always win out over a pessimist is beliefs. They might fail at first, but because they believe they will succeed, they try over and over until at last they claim victory in their lives. So many people blame their circumstances or their environment for where they are today. But in reality, it's their beliefs and the action they take on those beliefs that shape their destiny. No matter how old you are, how poor you are, or how much hardship you've been through, starting today you can change all that if you'll do one thing... believe. If you believe... there are no limits to your capabilities.

*Whether you believe you can achieve great things
or whether you believe you can't,
you're probably right.*

—*Henry Ford*

Unlimited Potential

If you limit your potential, you can bet that your chances for great achievement will remain limited! We've all heard many stories of ordinary people who have accomplished extraordinary feats, yet most people settle for watching others lead passionate lives while they sit passively on the sidelines. You might be wondering, why doesn't everyone take charge, set goals, and take control of their destiny? I've been asking this question all of my life. The answer is actually fairly simple. What holds people back from laying it all on the line and charging forth in pursuit of their dreams is their inability to take action. Most of the time, people's inability to take action comes from fear of failure. The pain of failure is enough to keep many frozen in their tracks. Often people opt to retreat and live out a life of mediocrity rather than strive for excellence. The irony is those people are shooting themselves in the foot. They have no idea of the power that lies sleeping inside them, that if harnessed, can take their lives to unimaginable levels of satisfaction and happiness.

There's one thing I do know about you... your desire to expand your horizons has brought you and me together. The fact that you've got this book in hand means that you are already taking action to improve the path you're on.

It's time to stop operating from a
system of limited beliefs . . .
It's time to stop operating out of fear . . .

Use Passion as Your Driving Force

Passion will convert apathy into conviction.
Passion will transform mediocrity into excellence.
Passion will drive you to overcome
insurmountable obstacles.

—*Andy Andrews*

Remember that feeling of certainty, that sense of total conviction when you were experiencing absolute passion for some one or some thing? All of us have had that feeling of passion in our lives at one time. When you are in that place of excitement, determination, and commitment, your brain starts looking for whatever way possible to achieve your goals. Maybe it seems like I'm stating the obvious, but it's the simple fundamentals that make all the difference. That's why great athletes go over the basics of their sport again and again. They have tremendous passion that drives them to continually push themselves to higher levels. Passion makes the difference between success and failure. Waking up each day without passion would be like trying to drive a car without gas. You're not going to get anywhere. On the other hand, if your pursuits are fueled with passion you will have the power to move mountains.

If you're searching for a new career or looking to make a fresh start, take a little time to think about the things that you're passionate about. Your career will take quantum leaps upward if you're passionate about your work. I've never met anyone who is successful in his field who isn't filled with enthusiasm for his work. The bottom line is **PASSION = SUCCESS!**

Unlimited Abundance

To have life more abundant,
we must think in limitless terms of abundance.
—*Thomas Dreier*

Traditional thinking says we live in a world of economic scarcity. Traditional thinking states that the best we can hope for is to divide up the pie differently because there's only so much to go around. But that's simply not true. *I grew up believing that my financial gain would be someone else's loss.* It was a true revelation when I discovered we live in a world of unlimited abundance. In economist Paul Zane Pilzer's book, *Unlimited Wealth*, he states:

> Through technology we now have resources which are being discovered faster than we can make use of them. Modern technology is transforming our most basic ideas about the creation of wealth. Traditional economics says that whoever controls the world's raw materials and essential commodities controls the world.

Mr. Pilzer persuasively argues that wealth is no longer produced by controlling scarce resources, because accelerating technological development has virtually eliminated scarcity. Where once Rockefeller or Carnegie got rich by controlling existing markets (oil and steel), today entrepreneurs Ross Perot and Sam Walton, in a new configuration Pilzer calls "economic alchemy," generate personal fortunes by providing products and services that did not exist before. The new economic alchemist does not find a need and then attempt to fill it; he creates demand by providing something newer, better, and, ultimately, necessary. God would not have created a world of limited resources in which one person's gain would have to be another person's loss. Surely He would allow everyone, not just a select few, to share in a better and better world.

For instance, since the 1930s, we have learned to reap one hundred times more crop yield from an acre of land. Because of technology we have learned to get twice the fuel efficiency from a gallon of gas. I remember when I bought my first car, a used 1964 Ford van. There was a gas shortage across the country with lines of cars stretching around the block. I remember thinking, "I wonder how I will ever be able to go on tour with the shortage of gas everywhere." Obviously we never ran out, but for a while there was a tremendous sense of scarcity and fear throughout the land.

A few years ago it dawned on me that I had always looked at wealth from a place of scarcity. Perhaps I was influenced by my grandparents, who had suffered through the Great Depression. Maybe I felt guilty at the thought of accumulating money. Maybe I was afraid it would be at the expense of others. None of these explanations could be further from the truth.

Embracing Change

We must realize that the only business that will endure is the business of change. The rules are changing every day, but if we embrace change it becomes our ally and greatest resource. For instance, as the owner of a recording complex, I have watched technology bring about affordable recording equipment, allowing many of my best clients the option to build their own home studios. In the last five years everything has begun to change. On one hand I'm watching the deterioration of the commercial recording studio business as I have known it, but on the other hand it's a powerful opportunity to expand my horizons by changing the way in which I offer value to my clients. Although it is critical that a world-class studio must strive to achieve technical excellence, that is no longer enough.

At Dark Horse Recording we have begun to view ourselves as more of a people business than a technical one, with an emphasis on finding better ways to service the needs of our clients. How can we pamper them and offer comforts that exceed their expectations? Conventional wisdom says to find a need and then fill it, but now we're learning to imagine what they might need and then create it. I learned this strategy when I read Lee Iacocca's autobiography. That's the same way he developed the Ford Mustang in the early 1960s. Instead of building a car in search of a market, he realized that there was a market in search of a car. The normal procedure in Detroit was to build a car and then try to identify its buyers. But Iacocca moved in the opposite direction and tailored the Mustang for a hungry new market, creating one of the biggest success stories in automotive history. During the first weekend it was on sale, an unprecedented four million people visited Ford dealerships. By the end of their first year they had sold 418,812 Mustangs. In the first two years alone, the Mustang generated net profits of $1.1 billion. And that was in 1964! Lee Iacocca had embraced the changing times. That success helped launch his career into the stratosphere where he continued to reinvent the way the automotive industry did business. If you ask Americans to name the most successful businessmen they can think of, Lee Iacocca is at the top of the list.

*We are wide-eyed in contemplating the possibility that
life may exist elsewhere in the universe,
but we wear blinders when contemplating the
possibilities of life on earth.*
—*Norman Cousins*

Unlimited Contribution

I cannot write a chapter about our unlimited potential without touching on the subject of contribution. The following text is merely a preface to my chapter "Remember the Higher Calling" which is dedicated to the principles of giving back a portion of the wonderful abundance we have been blessed with. As I have studied the principles of personal and professional success, I have realized that the most important key to having a life that is rich with joy is to learn the art of contribution. I believe as we create wealth, we have a responsibility to enrich the lives of others in the process. We are now living in a world of unlimited resources and wealth. We now have the capacity to create massive value where little existed before. This is how we can change the world. This is how we can help others and share in the unlimited abundance with which God has blessed us. This is how we can share God's blessings, by lifting up all those whom we have the privilege to touch.

*Only those who have learned the power of sincere
and selfless contribution experience life's
deepest joy: true fulfillment.*
—*Anthony Robbins*

14

THE JOY OF FINANCIAL ABUNDANCE

Money isn't everything...
and I wish I had a dollar for every time I said that.
— *Kirk Kirkpatrick*

The day that I started changing my outlook on money was the day that I began to enter into the flow of financial abundance. That simple distinction caused a chain of events that has brought about massive change and prosperity in my life.

Have you ever noticed how people have such strong reactions when the subject of money comes up? It's an emotionally charged issue for most of us. After all, it's simply a means of exchange allowing us to transfer and measure value we create with others. But while it excites some people, the thought of financial abundance infuriates others. They might feel money leads to lust and greed or that it is somehow evil. Often the people who have very little have contempt for those who have wealth. They say such things as, "All they ever think about is money." The truth is that when you are living hand-to-mouth, money can be all you think about.

That's how it was for me. For the first fifteen years of my adult life I struggled just to make it to the end of the month, and the foremost thought in my head was my lack of money. Growing up, I developed many negative connotations about wealth, most of them on a subconscious level.

> *The desire for gold is not for gold.*
> *It is the desire for the means of*
> *freedom and benefit.*
>
> —*Ralph Waldo Emerson*

Simply put, I had not conditioned myself for wealth. Outwardly I always worked hard to be a successful recording artist and performer, so why was I always just one month away from being out on the streets? What was holding me back? It wasn't that I was lazy; in fact, I was a borderline workaholic. I was always striving to earn more money, but my financial motivation was only fueled by the need to survive. Even as I was earning $3,000 a night for my concert performances, I was still living on nothing after paying enormous expenses for my crew and office staff. I began to realize that mentally I linked up things like greed, self-centeredness, envy, loneliness, anxiety, and stress to having money. How could I be motivated to accumulate wealth when I had that image?

Slowly I started changing those negative images for positive ones. Sure, there are rich people who are shallow and self-centered, but there are also affluent people who look on their wealth as a mission to help others. Take Dolly Parton, for instance. Do you know that she offers a

college scholarship to each and every person who gradu-
ates from high school in her hometown of Sevierville,
Tennessee?

> *The gratification of wealth is not found*
> *in mere possession or in lavish expenditure,*
> *but in its wise application.*
>   —*Miguel de Cervantes Saavedra*

There are countless examples of wealth being used
as a tool for good, for contribution, as a way to fuel
dreams and make a measurable difference in the world.
Having financial abundance began to take on a whole
new meaning for me. I realized that building wealth was
a worthy goal, not only for my family and me, but also
because it would enable me to contribute more to others.
For the first time in my life I committed to building
wealth, and almost overnight my finances began to
change. This is because I now had a sense of purpose
and a powerful "why."

If it's that simple, why don't most people succeed? We
live in one of the richest nations in the world where
abundance and opportunity surrounds us. What holds us
back?

> *There is only one success—to be able to*
> *spend your life in your own way.*
>   —*Christopher Morley*

If you want to earn more money, the answer is simple:
add more value. If you want to triple your income, triple
the amount of value you can add to your existing
employer. If you're self-employed, triple the amount of
value to your customers. This might sound overly simplis-

tic, but it's true. It's a fundamental truth that as you create ways to add value to others, your worth will begin to grow at an astounding rate.

For example, lately I've been shopping for furniture to upgrade the interior of my recording studios. There's one boutique I stumbled upon which had hot tea and coffee set out for its customers. When I walked in, a woman greeted me and asked if I'd like some fresh popcorn. Then she pointed to a display of every kind of candy bar and snack imaginable and offered me my choice. With a bag of popcorn in one hand and a cup of hot tea in the other, I began to look around the store, spending more time there than normal.

Although I didn't find what I was looking for, I have since caught myself dropping by a half dozen times. Anytime I'm shopping in that neighborhood I drop by, just in case they've gotten something in that might go well in one of the studios. I know, however, that I am actually drawn in by the warm smiles and inviting refreshments. Sooner or later I will purchase furniture there because they have added value to my shopping experience.

That's just one simple idea. Imagine how something like that could apply to your business. The possibilities are endless, and there are always creative ways to add value that cost little or no money.

Money doesn't always bring happiness.
People with ten million dollars are no happier
than people with nine million dollars.
—*Hobart Brown*

A large portion of the people on the *Forbes* Four Hundred List of the richest people in America started with little or no money. There are three and one-half million millionaires in the United States, and about 80 percent of those are first-generation affluent. Interestingly, their numbers are growing much faster than the general population. If you're asking if you can become one of them, the answer is yes. The attainment of wealth is not a mystical experience reserved for others. It's attainable and achievable for anyone who is willing to learn and apply the strategies that thousands of successful men and women use every day.

Know Your Outcome

It's simple—if you don't know what you're aiming for, how do you expect to hit the target? When I ask people what they want out of their careers, I'm often amazed to find out that they don't have any specific outcome in mind. These people find themselves vulnerable to whichever way the winds of change blow.

> *I have since met and spoken with many men and women who have achieved great success and they all had that one trait in common. They knew exactly what they wanted.*
>
> *—Brian Tracy*

This brings us to goal setting. It is tempting to write a whole chapter on the wonderful adventures you will have when you master the art of goal setting. In fact, it would be easy to turn that chapter into an entire book. This one thing can change your life dramatically. At first glance many people look on goal setting as an analytical and mind-numbing process for those with little imagination. Nothing could be further from the truth.

It's an opportunity to stretch your mind to new possibilities. This gives you a chance to let your imagination run wild, to brainstorm without limitations. It can be an incredible exercise. It can fuel ideas so compelling that your life will change as a result.

Learning to set goals turned my whole life around. It has helped transform every area of my life. In fact, it has become the road map that provides me with objectivity, clarity, and direction for my personal and professional life. For instance, while brainstorming about ways I could integrate speaking on personal development with my musical career, I came up with the idea of writing this book. Initially the whole idea seemed outrageous. Who was I to think that I could write a book that someone would want to read?

You see, I'm dyslexic, which means I have a neurological disorder that causes me to get numbers and letters backwards. To this day, I can't spell guitar without the help of my computer spell check. My literary skills were so bad that rather than fail me in English, my high-school teacher (who knew I was a handy woodworker) suggested a trade. He said he would pass me with a D if I would build him a podium to stand behind while he taught class. The night before final exams, instead of studying, I was in my garage crafting out that piece of furniture. I can still remember my mother watching me. She was shaking her head and smiling at the same time as if I was a boy only a mother could love.

I have never had much confidence in the area of reading and writing. Slowly, however, the preposterous idea of becoming an author sank in and became a tangible possibility, all because I wrote it down as a goal. Had it not been for setting goals, this book would have never become a reality. It has brought me the satisfaction of accomplishment, an outlet to express my ideas, and has provided me with another stream of income.

Don't underestimate the power of goals. They have provided a sense of clarity in my life that has brought about incredible results, and they will in yours as well.

> *Lead a life of your own design, on your terms—*
> *not one that others have scripted for you.*
> —Anthony Robbins

If you put yourself in a place of faith, high expectation, and a sense of certainty, you will become unstoppable at achieving whatever you put your mind to. A compelling goal will lift your sights and elevate you to higher standards of excellence in every area of your life. Don't take my word for it, ask those who are elderly what drives them. They'll probably tell you that they want to feel productive, that having things to look forward to energizes them to get up every day and stay active.

A study was done at Yale University in 1953 in which the graduating class was interviewed. They were asked about their goal-setting habits, and only 3% of the class responded that they had a written plan of clear, specific goals for the future. In 1973, twenty years later, that same graduating class was interviewed, and guess what? The 3% who had set goals were worth more financially than the other 97% of the class *combined*. They also reported themselves as happier, more well-adjusted, and more excited about their lives than the rest of the class. That's an amazing testament to the power of setting goals. That's the *measurable* power of goal setting.

The primary cause of success in life is the
ability to set and achieve goals.
That's why people who do not have goals
are doomed forever to work for those who do.
—*Brian Tracy*

A Sense of Purpose

It's critical to know the "why" behind your ambitions. Being able to define your purpose will fuel you with the motivation and drive it will take for you to follow through with your goals. This will help you turn dreams into reality—it will help you to creatively find solutions to accomplish seemingly overwhelming tasks. When a person has a strong enough sense of purpose, he becomes unstoppable.

When Nancy and I were first married she had a job, and I was doing quite well on the concert circuit. Our overhead was low, but then she was expecting and wanted to quit her job to be a full-time mother. I remember thinking, "How am I ever going to be able to figure out how to make ends meet?" Before we knew it, there were four children. I had a powerful "why" behind my need to make money. Now my oldest son, Andrew, is applying to colleges, and I can clearly envision a time in the near future when all four children will either be in private school or college. In the past, there was just myself to think about, but now meeting the needs of my family has given me the ultimate sense of purpose for creating wealth.

Maybe you want to be able to support worthy causes or start your own business. Perhaps you want to get out of debt, or build your dream home. A compelling sense of purpose is the major difference between simply having a dream and having a powerful reason to overcome the obstacles that will surely fall in your path along the way to achieving your goals.

Planning

There is nothing more satisfying than putting together a plan and seeing it through step by step. Studies have shown that for every hour you spend planning, you will save five hours of work. This lesson has taken me longer to learn than I care to admit. In my past, I had a pattern of being too eager to jump in and expend energy on a project that was not well planned out, but once I recognized this I shifted my focus to spending the lion's share of my time carefully planning out future projects. This has not only helped me to be more organized, but my rate of good-decision making has gone up tenfold.

Good planning is a bit like preparing to start a campfire. During the winter I enjoy building bonfires out on our property and sitting around the crackling flames with friends, enjoying the passage of time. But there's an art to starting a good fire. If you want a fire that's really going to ignite, you've got to lay the groundwork by stacking your kindling with plenty of breathing room between each piece of wood. Then it's critical that you have some dry leaves or small twigs to first help get things going. Once you've laid your groundwork, it's time to put the big wood on that's going to burn and give off heat for hours. By simply following this plan the mere strike of a match will turn a spark into a roaring fire.

Focus and Follow Through

When I was a teenager I remember my dad telling me, "You've got to learn to follow through." That was good advice. Back then I had a habit of fizzling out on my commitments. But I have since learned that the art of following through is a mindset that can be cultivated. Staying focused and following through for the three years it took to complete my newest studio was possibly the most challenging project I've ever undertaken. There were times that the overwhelming scope of the project, relative to my limited finances, brought me to my knees. I worked 80-90 hours a week with the construction crew as a builder and as a contractor, overseeing every detail and purchase. In the dead of winter and in the heat of summer there were times when I wished I'd never started such a mammoth project. It was extremely difficult to continually come up with the resources to keep moving ahead, but I did, and finally completed this marvelous dream. The rewards have been many.

> **If we all did the things we are capable of doing,**
> **we would literally astound ourselves.**
> —*Thomas Edison*

The satisfaction that has come from seeing this through has been exhilarating. If it burns to the ground tomorrow, I will still have with me the most important asset of this project. I will still have the lessons I learned about sticking to your dreams. Now I feel that I can accomplish anything. Of course, I can't finish talking about follow through without mentioning Thomas Edison once again. Remember, he made over 10,000 attempts before perfecting the incandescent light bulb! What incredible focus he had! We are all richer for his discovery.

Time Perspective

When the habits of financially successful people are studied, there is one thing they have in common: time perspective. The more a person stays focused on long-term objectives instead of short-term gain, the greater his success will be. For instance, an alcoholic might be thinking no further ahead than the next drink. But a success-conscious person is always thinking far into the future. Remember that the race is always judged by who comes through in the long run. That's a distinction that helped turn everything around for me. I'll be the first to say that it's hard to be thinking long term when you're living on the edge financially. But I began to solve this problem by dividing everything I did into two categories, short term and long term. My last album has taken me almost two years to complete. By continually focusing on long-term goals, I have been able to slow down, take my time, and cut no corners. Now I have just completed what I believe to be my best work by far, therefore giving me the greatest chance for success.

Excellence

Focus on excellence, not speed. If you make a commitment to excellence in every area of your life, financial abundance will be a natural outcome. We all admire an athlete or concert musician who strives for excellence.

We admire people like Arnold Schwarzenegger or Steven Spielberg because they strive for excellence in everything they do. As a guitarist I have a special appreciation for a well-crafted, hand-made guitar. Everyone appreciates a carefully crafted Swiss watch. Commitment to excellence is one of those qualities of character that are universally respected.

The quality of a person's life
is in direct proportion to one's commitment
to excellence.

If you develop these qualities and follow this outline, you will not only become unstoppable in achieving financial goals, but you will also gain high levels of self-confidence and inner satisfaction. Become a creator of circumstance and add value to others, and you will succeed beyond your wildest dreams.

The Higher Calling

Once again, don't forget the higher calling when you become a creator of wealth. All the money in the world means nothing if you keep it for yourself. I'll paraphrase the parable of the talents found in Matthew 25:14 to illustrate how we should invest what we've been given wisely. Jesus told a story of a man going on a journey who entrusts his property to three of his servants. To the first he gives five talents (a measure of money), to the next he gives two talents, and to the third one talent, each according to his ability. Then he departs. After a long time the master returns and gathers his servants together to settle accounts with them. The man who received the five talents had put his money to work and gained five more. His master replied, "Well done, good and faithful servant! You have been faithful with the things I entrusted you, now I will put you in charge of much more." The next man came forth and said, "You entrusted me with two talents and I have gained two more." His master replied, "Well done, good and faithful servant! You have been faithful with a few things, now I will put you in charge of many things." Then the man who had been given the one talent came forward and said, "Master, I knew that you were a hard man, so I was afraid and went out and hid your talent in the ground. See, here is what belongs to you." His master replied, "You wicked and lazy servant! Take the talent from him and give it to the one who has ten. Everyone who is faithful with what I entrusted him will have abundance."

The point to this story is obvious: those who are good stewards with what they've been given will be put in charge of much more.

If we look at creating wealth as a mission and a tool for good, then we are "in the zone" to make a difference in the world... and we will truly experience the ultimate joy financial abundance can bring.

The extent to which one understands the principles of creating wealth is the extent to which he will become wealthy. Becoming wealthy starts with having a wealthy mindset. On a subconscious level, most people are not willing to be wealthy because of predisposed attitudes and conditioning. Nobody can begin to build real wealth until they've mastered the true source of wealth—their own mind. Truly wealthy people do not worry about acquiring money because they know that wherever it comes from, there is an inexhaustible supply of it.

It always helps me to remember that the rich and the poor have the same twenty-fours each day with which to work. The sun shines on the poor and the rich—and the rain pours on the poor and the rich as well.

15

THEY'RE NOT LAUGHING NOW

Let me tell you 'bout a girl I knew
A pudgy girl back in school
She had greasy hair and geeky glasses
The object of ridicule
The other day in the check out line
They were ringing up my rice and beans
There she was, a pretty little face
On the cover of a magazine
Just goes to show that you never know
Just what tomorrow may bring
See life is Curious Thing

"Curious Thing"
lyrics by Amy Grant & Wayne Kirkpatrick
(Amy Grant)

No one likes to be laughed at. Many times people don't venture out in pursuit of their dreams because they're afraid of what others may say. They're afraid of being laughed at. There's nothing more inspiring than stories about people who went against the odds, and, even when others were laughing at them, forged ahead and achieved greatness. In this chapter are a few of the stories that give me that extra dose of inner strength and courage to keep on keeping on when times get tough.

The Italian Stallion

Do you know that Sylvester Stallone was accidentally injured during birth when the doctor's forceps severed a facial nerve? Do you know that his early years were spent with a caregiver in a boarding house in Queens, seeing his parents only on weekends? Do you know that by the time he was 15, he had been in and out of 12 different schools and expelled from several of them? Do you know that he was turned down by literally hundreds of agents before the world knew him as the creator, screenwriter, and star of *Rocky*? Stallone says that in the early days he wouldn't take a day job even when he was down to his last dollar, because he feared it would lead to complacency about his desire to be an actor. He knew he had to burn his bridges to ensure that he had no choice but to find acting work. *That's a strong example of self-imposed leverage, which is such a powerful way to help people follow through with their plans.* At one point he turned to writing screenplays. In order to focus better, he painted his windows black.

After seeing a boxing match one night he sat down and for twenty hours straight sketched out a rough draft of the script for *Rocky*. The story goes that during the time he was shopping his new movie script, he was totally broke—so broke that in order to survive he sold his dog for $25. Eventually he received an offer of $125,000, but turned it down because they wouldn't accept his condition to be the star of the film. Imagine turning down that much money if you were totally broke! Imagine how intense his focus and vision must have been to make that decision! They countered with an offer of $250,000, but he still turned it down. They came back with an offer of $325,000. Again he turned it down. He absolutely insisted that he should star in this movie. Finally they agreed to give him a chance, but under the condition that he settle for just $35,000, a fraction of his earlier offers. What do you think the first thing he did with his money was? He went back to the exact location where he had originally sold his dog in the hopes that he might somehow spot the man who bought him. After several days of waiting he did see him and offered $50 for his dog. But the man wouldn't even consider it. Stallone doubled his offer, but the man had become attached to this dog and wasn't interested. Sylvester kept upping the offer with no luck. Finally, he agreed to pay $15,000 plus give the man a small part in his new film, *Rocky*! Well, as they say, the rest is history. The film was nominated for three Academy Awards and won Best Picture of 1976, and Sylvester proved that he could confront adversity and prevail. The character of Rocky is heroic—the underdog who struggles against the odds until he triumphs. It's a story we can all relate to. If the story ended here that would be enough, but for Sylvester Stallone it would be just the tip of the iceberg.

To date, Stallone has starred in over twenty movies. His *Rocky* and *Rambo* series alone have grossed nearly **$2 billion**. He has become one of America's hottest export stars. In 1995, he signed a record $60 million, three-movie film deal with Universal Studios. No one's laughing at Sly now.

My struggle in life, like that of many people,
is to have some control over my destiny,
to succeed or fail on my own terms,
to be given the chance to go the distance.

— *Sylvester Stallone*

I'll Be Back

Goals are dreams we convert to plans
and take action to fulfill.

— *Zig Ziglar*

Imagine becoming so successful that you have a stadium named after you in your hometown of Graz, Austria. Imagine becoming Mr. Universe by the age of 20 and then going on to win an unprecedented 13 world titles in bodybuilding. Imagine coming to America determined to be a movie star. Sound ridiculous? Imagine becoming one of the most successful and highly paid movie stars of all time. Unless you've been hiding under a rock, you know the phrase, "I'll be back." It was coined by Arnold Schwarzenegger, a man whose accomplishments have become legendary. His movies have become a part of American culture, and he is considered one of the most famous men in the world. He has written numerous books on health and fitness. On top of all that he has served as the weight training coach for the Special Olympics and has been Executive Commissioner of the Hollenbeck Innercity Games in Los Angeles—a mini-Olympics designed to help kids say "No" to drugs and violence, and "Yes" to fitness as a way of life. He also served as chairman of the President's Council on Physical Fitness and Sports.

When Arnold first came to Hollywood to break into show business, he was told he had everything going against him starting with his almost impossible-to-pronounce name. Even after his first couple of movie roles, people laughed at his thick accent and muscle-bound body, but his positive attitude, burning desire, and fierce determination made all the difference. He turned a career that could have become a lemon into lemonade, and no one's laughing now.

> *Men are born to succeed,*
> *not to fail.*
> —*Henry David Thoreau*

Going for the Gold

> *Success is simply a matter of luck.*
> *Ask any failure.*
> —*Earl Wilson*

At the age of 29, I moved to Nashville feeling frustrated and unsure of myself. After ten years as a professional musician I was still struggling to make ends meet... in fact, I was dead broke. I was questioning whether I had any business continuing, and was starting to believe the only reason I had survived this long in the music industry was that I had learned to live on nothing. It seemed that everytime things would begin to take off, I experienced a major setback... as Bruce Springsteen would say, "One step up, two steps back." Although times were hard, I did manage to sign a new recording contract with a small jazz label within the first six months of living in Nashville. In preparation to begin recording my next album, I spent every day in my small efficiency apartment writing and rehearsing. It just so happened that the summer Olympics were in progress. While I practiced and wrote, I would keep my little black-and-white TV on for company.

> *There are two things people want*
> *more than sex and money...*
> *recognition and praise.*
>
> —*Mary Kay Ash*

Every day the networks would run stories about Americans who were pushing their limits for the dream of participating in the Olympics. It was inspiring to hear their stories... For instance, a runner woke up at 3:00 in the morning and worked out for four hours, went off to work, then returned home and put in another three hours each evening. A female gymnast trained for years dreaming of who she would become if she could compete for the gold. I thought to myself, "Where do these people find the drive and inspiration to put in this kind of commitment?" Imagine putting everything on the line for the outside chance that they would participate in the Olympics... to challenge themselves to such high levels of excellence? The possible fame and fortune these people might receive from winning would be great, but more important was the personal satisfaction and self-confidence that came from that level of discipline and commitment. Those stories were a tremendous source of encouragement and literally kept me going that summer. *For people who take on these kinds of challenges, life-changing experiences occur as they push against their limitations.*

You measure the size of the accomplishment
by the obstacles you had to
overcome to reach your goals.
                    —*Booker T. Washington*

Oprah and Laura— Marathon Women

What do my sister, Laura Runge, and
Oprah Winfrey have in common?
They both ran the 26-mile marathon!

Recently I rented a video about Oprah Winfrey's fight and triumph with staying fit called *Make the Connection*. What a powerful and encouraging story it is for anyone who is trying to overcome personal challenges! As you may know, Oprah has had a life-long battle with her weight and eating habits, and she has shared those struggles on TV in front of millions. By sharing her own experiences and vulnerabilities, she has helped others, letting others know that they are not alone. For years, she roller-coastered, losing as much as 50 or 60 pounds and then putting the weight back on. The last straw came the night of the 1992 Daytime Emmy Awards. She was sitting in the audience, secretly hoping she wouldn't win the Emmy for Best Talk-Show Host because that would mean she would have to walk up on stage—all 237 pounds of her. She did win, and found her own personal nightmare staring her in the face with millions of people watching. Oprah realized that she had finally hit bottom and was willing to do absolutely anything to gain control of her weight problem.

A person sooner or later discovers that
they are the master gardener of their soul,
the director of their life.

—*James Allen*

In 1993, Oprah met Bob Greene, an exercise physiologist who put her on the path to victory. Besides showing her new ways to exercise and eat, more importantly he helped her adjust her attitude toward eating and exercising. What he taught her was that losing weight and keeping it off was a matter of changing her beliefs and behaviors. She learned to identify and change her patterns of unhealthy eating that were rooted in negative emotions, such as feeling neglected or abandoned, and those that were rooted in negative behaviors, such as being unable to say no to rich foods when dining out with friends. It didn't happen overnight, but as she consistently strove to break old patterns and develop new ones, her life was changed forever.

In this book I have spent a lot of time discussing the power of thought. In Oprah's case, the key for positive and permanent change was a mental realization. This does not detract from the fact that she has worked her buns off (literally) with tremendous discipline and determination. But it was her thoughts that preceded the actions. She went on to change the way she thought about eating vegetables and fresh fruit instead of the fried foods she loved. She learned to drink water even though she hates it. She changed the way she thought about sweating when exercising. As her attitude changed toward diet and exercise, her actions followed suit.

Consistency was the most important key to her transformation. Daily she followed through with her plan for a healthy body, and that consistency brought about amazing results. In time, Oprah began to experience changes in her life that went beyond merely losing weight. She experienced the joy and satisfaction of being in control of her physical wellbeing. She says, "I didn't know it was possible to feel so good."

Guess what? A year and a half after she met Bob Greene, she not only had lost eighty-seven pounds, but she also ran a 26-mile marathon and finished! Oprah said that finishing that race is the greatest victory of her life.

> *Success is determined by taking*
> *the hand you were dealt and*
> *utilizing it to the very best of your ability.*
>
> — *Ty Boyd*

On a similar note, my sister Laura recently ran a 26-mile marathon which required almost a year of training. What makes this story doubly inspiring to me is that Laura is not a natural runner. You might say she was running against the wind. Through a Dallas branch of the national fitness program, USA FIT, she committed to working out five days a week. With determination like a freight train, day in and day out she consistently began her morning training at 4:30 a.m., where she would run for miles before she went off to work. On Saturdays, she participated in a long distance group run regardless of soaring Texas temperatures or inclement weather. She puts in unusually long hours at work and could rightfully have every excuse to renege on her commitment, but she never did. Her friends thought she was crazy... why would she put herself through all that torture? After setbacks and pulled muscles, the big day came; and she not only started that overwhelming run, she finished! This reminds me of the story of the tortoise and the hare.

As you know, the tortoise was not an impressive runner, but he was consistent and, in the long run, won the race! The rewards of Laura's accomplishment go way beyond developing running skills. She has built character and confidence that affect every aspect of her life. Laura has been echoing Oprah's sentiments as to how vibrant she feels. She has a new sense of certainty that she can achieve anything she puts her mind to.

According to *Forbes* magazine, Oprah is soon to become the country's first African-American billionaire. But all that money could not magically make her physically fit. That's something she had to earn—the same as Laura or anyone else. Their conviction, commitment, and hard work have been glowing examples of human triumph.

A Night At The Movies

My two oldest sons and I are real movie buffs, so when the Academy Awards are held each year it always becomes a family event. In 1999, *Titanic* won 11 Oscars, including best picture, and director James Cameron took home three of them himself. It's no secret that Cameron can be difficult to work with because of the high level of perfection he demands. But I really appreciate his commitment to excellence. He had to overcome enormous adversities to get the picture done. I remember reading all kinds of gossip about his out-of-control budget and his obsessive attitude toward getting that picture done at all costs. Critics were predicting that the enormous budget ($200 million) was somehow a foretelling of an epic disaster. Many believed the picture would sink just like the ship. Of course, you know the rest of the story. *Titanic* is one of the biggest successes of all time, taking home more awards and grossing more income than any other movie in history. The worldwide box office gross is now approaching a staggering two billion dollars. Cameron created what is sure to be one of the classic films of all time.

By far the most inspiring story of the evening to me was the huge success of Matt Damon and Ben Affleck, a couple of twenty-somethings who won the Oscar for best original screenplay for *Good Will Hunting,* starring Robin Williams and Matt Damon. Imagine teaming up with a childhood friend and having this kind of success with a movie script written in college. The finished draft, which Damon co-wrote with Affleck, had drawn the interest of several studios, but no one wanted to produce it with them in the lead roles. They stuck to their guns and refused several lucrative offers until Castle Rock finally bought the rights to *Good Will Hunting.* Before it was all over, Miramax acquired the script and the rest is history. *Good Will Hunting* grossed $138 million in the U.S. alone!

Jump!

While I lived in California, I formed a band to showcase my songs with the high hopes of landing a recording contract. We showcased throughout the Los Angeles area hoping to be discovered... and to keep food on the table we played local clubs. One time when we were really broke, we took a six-week gig in a club in Alaska. Another time we landed a tour opening for the Atlanta Rhythm Section, playing mostly small coliseums and large gymnasiums through the Midwest. Almost daily we rehearsed in an empty warehouse in Watts, where we constantly crafted our songs and our live performance. Jim Ingle was my partner and band mate. He was always the first one to arrive at rehearsal, he had a great attitude during even the toughest of times, and he was professional to a fault. Over the four years we worked together, he was constantly finding ways to improve not only his drumming and singing skills, but his visual performance as well. Over time he began to stand out from the pack with his blend of creative, rock-solid style and striking showmanship. You couldn't take your eyes off him. Whether we were playing at a small club where no one seemed to even pay attention or in front of thousands, he always gave 110 percent.

The price of success is much lower
than the price of failure.

Every musician playing in a band shares pretty much the same dream: to become a member of a hit act, tour the world traveling first class, perform in front of thousands of people a night, and get paid lots of money for it! It's what drives many hopeful musicians to put up with ridiculous obstacles such as living in poverty, dealing with constant rejection, playing in all kinds of undesirable places, and working all kinds of undesirable hours. Of all the musicians I worked with during my time in California, Jim is the only one who went on to live out the rock-and-roll fantasy.

The more lines of preparation…
The greater the chance of intersecting
the line of opportunity.

During the 1980s, there seemed to be literally thousands of bands in Los Angeles, all with the same goal—to land a major record deal. As for our band, after four years we finally decided that we had given it our best shot and that it was time for each of us to move on. That's when I left LA for good.

About one year later, Jim had an incredible opportunity to audition for the Pointer Sisters. He showed up at a Los Angeles soundstage along with a handful of other drummers, all hoping to be to chosen to hold the groove for one of the hottest acts of the decade. Initially, another drummer was chosen for the position, but a few weeks later Jim got a call saying they wanted to hear him again. But for this second audition there was some added pressure. Because the group was in the middle of a national tour and because of the sudden absence of their existing drummer, **Jim's audition was to be an entire live concert performance with the Pointer Sisters!** A tape of the show was sent to him, and he had only about 48 hours to listen as he prepared to get himself and his drums up to Valley Forge, Pennsylvania, where they would be performing in the round at the Valley Forge Music Fair. The rest was up to him. This was at a time when their album *Break Out* was storming up the charts, fueled by the enormous success of their hit single, "*Jump,*" so the pressure was really on.

Imagine having to lay it all on the line in front of thousands of people who had bought tickets expecting a flawless performance. But Jim was prepared. All year he had been practicing endlessly in order to be ready whenever opportunity finally knocked. He was already a killer drummer, but he still spent countless hours developing his ability to hold down a rock-steady groove— essential when you're the driving force behind the rhythmic dance music of a group like the Pointer Sisters. He had also outfitted his drums with flight cases just in case something ever came up and he needed to fly his gear across the country. Something came up all right, and it changed the course of his life. Not only did Jim pass the audition, but he kept his gig with the Pointers for fourteen years, traveling and performing all over the world. Just one month after his audition, the Pointers were presented two American Music Awards, sending their popularity into orbit. They were now playing nothing but the biggest and most prestigious venues. They had become one of the most successful headlining acts in the world, and Jim was a part of it!

I remember seeing all this for the first time when they came to Nashville. At one point in the show, Jim was featured playing an extended drum solo. There he was, in front of over ten thousand people, with his pounding rhythms sounding out over the huge concert speakers as dozens of spotlights focused on him, and I stood there thinking, "Way to go, Jim!"

Was it luck that got him that sought-after position? I don't think so. I believe it was a combination of many things working together:

- ♦ *Determination*
  - ♦ *Desire*
    - ♦ *Diligence*
      - ♦ *Perseverance*
        - ♦ *Preparation*
          - ♦ *Professionalism*
            - ♦ *Consistency*
              - ♦ *Integrity*
                - ♦ *Talent*

Notice I put talent at the end of the list. This is not to take away from Jim's extraordinary musical ability, but simply to point out that without these other qualities it's quite likely that Jim would still be one of thousands of other drummers in LA who are wondering why they haven't gotten their big break. He once told me, "Everyone will have an opportunity cross their path sooner or later, but the key is to be prepared."

Pink Cadillac

You are probably asking yourself, "Wasn't 'Pink Cadillac' a song by Bruce Springsteen and Aretha Franklin? Or was it a movie by Clint Eastwood?" You are right on all counts, but when I hear those words, the first image that comes to mind is Mary Kay Ash awarding pink Cadillacs to her top salespeople.

There's nothing more exciting than to see someone start with humble beginnings and beat the odds, rise far above the limitations that others have set and go on to a level of tremendous success. Mary Kay has done just that. I first heard her story on *Sixty Minutes* several years back. It was inspiring to see where she came from and where she is now.

She grew up very poor; in fact, at the age of seven she was taking care of her sick father and household duties while her mother worked to support the family. She was married at 17, the mother of three children at 24, and at 20 began helping to supplement the family's income, first by selling children's books and, later, housewares. She discovered a natural ability for sales, which was fortunate, because her husband requested a divorce after his return from service in World War II, and she became her children's sole financial supporter. In 1963, when Mary Kay was 45 years old, she found herself suddenly alone. Her three children were grown, and her husband of three years had just died of a heart attack. With an investment of only $5,000, she threw herself into her dream: a direct sales company run by women for women, featuring a unique line of skin-care products she believed would sell themselves. She rented a small storefront in Dallas and filled boxes with jars labeled "Beauty by Mary Kay." Her two sons helped her. Ben Rogers contributed $4,500 from his savings, and Richard Rogers quit his job and began selling life insurance to pay the bills while he helped his mom. They began to build what would become an empire.

Consider that at this time in her life she could have succumbed to grief. She felt depressed and defeated and was having trouble finding a reason to get out of bed each day. Instead, she chose to do something she believed in despite the opinion of others, including her attorney, that her company would fail. She reached out to family and friends and began a new life on her terms.

Over the next decade Mary Kay went on to achieve the impossible. Defying all the nay-sayers, her products slowly but surely caught on in the Dallas area. She was going up against companies like Avon, which had seventy-seven years of experience in the direct sales cosmetics market. Nonetheless, her company grew throughout the 1960s. The annual sales seminars grew from humble homemade dinners into increasingly lavish extravaganzas. Each year hundreds, and then thousands, of women convened in Dallas to attend classes and hear motivational speakers. The highlight is awards night when she recognizes top sales consultants, ascending Mary Kay's "Ladder of Success." Each rung brings a new badge of honor starting with ribbons, then sashes, badges, lapel bars, diamond bracelets, bumblebee pins, and, of course, the ultimate honor, a pink Cadillac.

The positive thinker sees the invisible,
feels the intangible,
and achieves the impossible.

Today, Mary Kay Cosmetics has more than 425,000 sales consultants worldwide and boasts annual sales of over $950 million.

I wasn't interested in the dollars and cents
part of the business;
my interest in 1963 was in offering women
opportunities that didn't exist anywhere else.
—*Mary Kay Ash*

She likes to wear a diamond lapel pin shaped like a bumblebee, pointing out, "Aerodynamics have proven that the bumblebee cannot fly. The body is too heavy and the wings are too weak. But the bumblebee doesn't know that, and it goes right on flying, miraculously." Maybe that's the perfect metaphor for this extraordinary woman who kick-started a small business dream into reality, going against all odds.

Man of Imagination

Our thoughts and imaginations are the
only real limits to our possibilities.
—*Orison Swett Marden*

I believe each one of us has the ability to tap into our own vast imagination. You have only to observe children at play to realize that all of us were born with keen imaginations. As I watch my two youngest children

(Savana, three years, and Nakota, six years), it never ceases to amaze me how their imaginations seem to have no limits. They can find an endless number of things to do with a cardboard box, or they'll invent dozens of ways to jump off the bed. They come up with hilarious names for imaginary pets. They invent new ways to play "Hide and Go Seek." They're unconcerned about rules and restrictions. Every object, every action, is a fresh and new experience for them. I find myself learning life lessons from them, remembering that with a little imagination there are unlimited possibilities at every turn.

When anyone hears the name Walt Disney, words like imagination and creativity come to mind. As a child, he passed away the hours drawing cartoon characters and creating imaginary friends. In 1920, he signed on at $40 per week as an illustrator with the Kansas City Film Ad Company, which made 60-second animated cartoon advertisements that were screened in theaters. He was only nineteen then, and by the time he was twenty-two he was heading off to Hollywood because he heard that young filmmakers could find financial backing for their projects. This is only one of the many times he **jumped... and the net appeared.** That doesn't mean Disney didn't endure setbacks and hardships. In fact, he dealt with adversity often. When he first moved to Hollywood, he had nothing more to offer than imagination and ambition.

> *Imagination is more important*
> *than knowledge.*
>
> —*Albert Einstein*

At first he couldn't find work, so Disney did what he'd done under the same circumstances in Kansas City: he became an entrepreneur. As he put it, "When you can't get a job, you start your own business." He soon came up with a cartoon character he called Mickey Mouse. His imagination kept him at the forefront of advancing technology. In 1927, he saw the premiere of *The Jazz Singer*, the first film to synchronize sound with action, which convinced him that Mickey would have to be heard as well as seen. He produced *Steamboat Willie*, which became an overwhelming undertaking. He insisted that the sound be in perfect synchronization with the moving pictures. He hired a full orchestra to record the music and produced almost 20,000 handcrafted frames, the most used to date for an animation project. His company was running out of money, and in an effort to stay afloat Disney sold his prized sports car. He mortgaged everything he had and came up with the $15,000 needed to produce the sophisticated cartoon. He had taken a leap of faith that paid off—*Steamboat Willie* became a huge success, and Disney was now in demand. He began turning out a new Mickey Mouse feature each month. Universal Studios, as well as several others, made offers to handle Disney's distribution—and even buy his company outright. But Disney, who once said, "I wanted to retain my individuality," wasn't interested in being acquired. Although Mickey Mouse was making a fortune, his expenses were eating up the profits. No matter how hard times got, Disney held on to his copyrights. "Mickey Mouse to me is the symbol of independence," he once said. By 1930, Mickey had become a worldwide phenomenon. Disney continued to expand his marketing horizons with *The Mickey Mouse Book* and the Mickey Mouse watch. The watch sold 2.5 million units in its first two years. Disney created the first cartoon ever filmed in Technicolor, *Flowers and Trees*, which won the first of 48 Oscars the studio would receive in his lifetime. He continued to take chances and expand his vision. He saw his studio as an "idea factory."

In 1938, Disney released the first full-length animated feature film, *Snow White and the Seven Dwarfs*. Because of his high standards for excellence, the budget went spiraling past the initial $250,000 to over a million dollars. Once again, he received scorn from a chorus of nay-sayers who called it "Disney's Folly."

Disney remembers, "We had decided there was only one way we could successfully do *Snow White*. It was to go for broke, shoot the works. There could be no compromise on money, talent, or time."

When the movie debuted, audiences all across the country flocked to theaters. *Snow White* was a huge success, and in no time brought in $8.5 million on its first release—and it's been earning money ever since. In fact, in the United States alone, it was re-released six times by 1993, and to date has been distributed in forty-six countries, grossing over $100 million dollars!

As he continued to expand, Disney took one risk after another, never willing to sacrifice quality. By 1940, he had accumulated $4.5 million in debt. Upon going public to raise funds, he created *Pinocchio* and *Bambi*, then in 1942, *Fantasia*, Disney's most ambitious feature to date. It seemed as if his imagination had no limits. When World War II hit, Disney applied the fruits of his imagination to the war effort. He produced animated instructional films, including one called *The New Spirit*, in which Donald Duck talked about the need to pay income taxes on time.

By the end of the war, Disney was again deeply in debt, but his vivid imagination came to the rescue. He started producing documentary films, with wild animals as the stars, in a series called *True Life Adventure*. His first one, *Sea Island,* won an Academy Award for best documentary and was a hit at the box office. For the following years he was still scraping by financially, but his creativity and imagination never slowed down. Disney went on to sign an exclusive long-term contract with ABC, and created the *Wonderful World of Disney* television show, hosted by Walt Disney and featuring cartoons and nature films. It was an enormous hit as 31 million of the 75 million possible viewers tuned in. I was one of them. My best television memories are sitting in front of the TV on Sunday nights watching the *Wonderful World of Disney* with my family. The following year he created *The Mickey Mouse Club,* a new type of television show that appealed to seemingly everyone. During the show's peak popularity in the mid-1950s, Mickey Mouse ears sold at a rate of 25,000 sets per day!

Did you know that Disneyland in California is the world's first theme park? The story goes that Disney got the idea while watching his two daughters play on a merry-go-round.

"I felt that there should be something built, some kind of family park, where parents and children could have fun together," he recalled.

That thought was the seed of a vision that eventually became a worldwide phenomenon, providing clean family entertainment for millions, and employing tens of thousands of people as well—Disney theme parks!

Because his stockholders were hesitant to cooperate, Disney started his own separate company to plan the theme park venture and took the risk of investing his entire life savings in launching it. But he still needed other backers. Before Walt Disney found financing for Disneyland, a staggering 403 banks turned him down. What if he had given up at bank number 402? The world would have surely lost out on a great treasure. The first day Disneyland opened in 1955, it was an instant sensation. In fact, during that first, week over 170,000 people visited the park.

The story of how Disney's imagination produced so many wonderful things is amazing. It's also interesting how other people's lack of imagination failed to hold his ideas back. Because of his vision, determination, desire, persistence, and, of course, imagination, the world will never be the same.

> *It's a sticky situation*
> *when I'm near hallucination,*
> *And I refuse to bow.*
> *They used to think me funny*
> *when I promised them their money,*
> *But they're not laughing now*
> *"Gift with a Golden Gun"*
> *lyrics by David Paich and Bobby Kimball*
> *(Toto)*

16

REMEMBER THE HIGHER CALLING

I'm gonna make a change, for once in my life
It's gonna feel real good, gonna make a difference
Gonna make it right . . .
I'm starting with the man in the mirror
I'm asking him to change his ways
And no message could have been any clearer
If you wanna make the world a better place
Take a look at yourself, and then make a change

"Man in the Mirror"
lyrics by Garrett and Ballard
(Michael Jackson)

The Fruits of Contribution

There is an award for humanitarian efforts that is given by the National Association of Campus Activities. It's called the Harry Chapin Award and it honors the efforts of Harry Chapin, the singer/songwriter whose life was tragically interrupted in a fatal car wreck, but who left a legacy of activism fighting hunger and poverty. "The Cat's in the Cradle" and "Taxi" are two of his most famous songs. The award is usually given out to someone in the entertainment industry, (for instance in earlier years it was given to Jackson Browne and Kenny Rogers), but several years back it was awarded to President Jimmy Carter as well. In 1996, I was given this award for the small part I have played as a warrior in the fight against Third World poverty. For over a decade this has been my passion, my mission, and my quest. My efforts have been funneled through Compassion International, a Christian organization sponsoring over 100,000 children in the U.S. and other countries around the world. Every once in a while a college will bring me in for a concert because they want to put on a fundraiser to raise awareness of the plight of impoverished children. They know that I will be able to tie my performance in with their efforts. Upon receiving this award I was invited to give some concerts sponsored by Arizona Western College. They asked if I could come in for five days and perform at a half dozen high schools in the southern part of the state. This was a program the college sponsored as an arts enrichment outreach to the community, particularly to underprivileged schools. The students who attend these schools are the children of migrant workers, many of whom live in camps set up outside dusty little towns along the Arizona-Mexico border.

The best thing these students have going for them is their chance for an education, a privilege that often goes unappreciated by many Americans. Even though located in the United States, some of these schools were as rundown and dilapidated as those in poorer countries because of lack of funds. But the students were great!

They were enthusiastic and appreciative to have someone come in to perform for them.

> *Try not to become a man of success,*
> *but rather a man of value.*
> —*Albert Einstein*

Dust & Dirt

During my five-day stay, I was taken to a little orphanage in the town of San Luis, Mexico, just across the border from Yuma, Arizona. The forty or fifty children living in Bethel Orfanatorio were at the bottom of the already crumbling social ladder. They had absolutely nothing. The orphanage had no funding except for donations and volunteer help. As we drove through the streets of San Luis, the roads, houses, and yards were completely covered with dust. It was bleak and surreal. Never had I seen anything like this, even in my visit to Haiti. As we pulled up to the orphanage, there were the children, sitting around a couple of picnic tables. This was their playground; not one blade of grass anywhere, just dust and dirt.

> **Success has nothing to do with what you gain in life or accomplish for yourself. It's what you do for others.**
> —*Danny Thomas*

Our plan was to find out what food they might need and head off to the local market, load up, and return with the goods. The challenge was that none of them could speak English, and we couldn't speak Spanish. After a few minutes of gesturing, several of the young women got in our van and pointed the way to a Mexican supermarket.

It was a bit like the ones here in the States, but they had many of the essential foods in bulk. Of course, I couldn't read the labels or comprehend the pricing. At first, I suspected these women would take advantage of me and point toward the most expensive foods, but nothing could have been further from the truth. We found our way to the produce area, and they put perhaps a dozen apples into our cart. Then I added four dozen more because, after all, there were forty mouths to feed. They scooped five pounds of rice into a bag, then I motioned to the clerk to bring us a fifty-pound bag from the back room. This went on for a couple of hours, until one of the girls had tears in her eyes. It was becoming obvious how much the supplies, which we take for granted, were desperately needed. They were interested only in the absolute essentials. I kept thinking, "Let's get some soda pop or other fun food for the kids." But they were operating at a survival level I didn't really understand. By the time we had finished, we had seven shopping carts filled to the brim. After much difficulty in getting checked out and paying the bill, we loaded up the van and headed back to the orphanage.

She calls out to the man on the street
Sir can you help me?
It's cold, and I've nowhere to sleep
Is there somewhere can you tell me?
He walks on and he doesn't look back
He pretends he can't hear her
Starts to whistle as he crosses the street
Seems embarrassed to be there
Oh think twice, it's just another day
for you and me in paradise

"Another Day In Paradise"
lyrics by Phil Collins

It was about 10:00 p.m. when we returned, and the children had bedded down for the night. The three older adults watching over things began helping us unload. You could see their gratitude by the smiles on their faces. This is when reality started setting in for me. As we began bringing the groceries into the small, stark kitchen it hit me—**there was no food anywhere!**

Did those children go to bed hungry?
What would they have had for breakfast?
Where would they find food for the next week?

Once the groceries had been unpacked, the two young women led me to a series of cinderblock rooms with cots lined up along the walls. The children, some as young as three and four, were huddled together two and three to a bed. It was cold, and half of them had no blankets. It tore my heart out. As the father of four, I can hardly imagine how a young child survives without nurturing parents there to comfort him at every moment. These children had no one to hold them while they fell asleep or when they woke up crying after a bad dream. It was overwhelming.

That night, as I headed back to my warm, comfortable hotel room in Yuma, my heart was pounding with conflicting emotions.

I was embarrassed.
How could I ever complain about anything again?
How could I return to my fabulous home and ignore this need?
What could I do to make a difference?

I knew I had just had one of the richest experiences life has to offer... helping others one on one at a basic survival level. I've raised hundreds of thousands of dollars for the poor, but only when I experienced their plight could I feel their pain. Mother Teresa described this as "the face of poverty." As we take charge of our lives, let us think beyond the pursuit of wealth. Let us adjust our attitudes so that we see wealth as a *means for contribution*. We live in a country where anything is possible. We can take charge of our own lives, and we can make a difference in the lives of those around us. Let's live with a sense of mission and purpose... a strong desire to make a difference.

> *Many persons have a wrong idea of what*
> *constitutes true happiness.*
> *It is not attained through self-gratification, but*
> *through fidelity to a worthy purpose.*
> —Helen Keller

When we slow down and take stock of our lives, there can be no doubt that God has blessed us beyond measure—especially those of us who live in America. Not only do we live in a free country, but also in a land of unlimited possibilities. With encouragement, almost any child can rise up and achieve a life of extraordinary results. If you are reading this book, I am going to assume that you have much for which to be grateful. Do not forget to cultivate an attitude of gratitude! Those who have been given more carry with them the privilege and the responsibility to be good stewards of these blessings. We all know that when we reach out and give of ourselves, we receive the richest blessing of all... a sense of meaning and purpose during our stay in this world.

The great use of life is to spend it for
something that will outlast it.
—*William James*

As I've said before, if humans are the only creatures on the planet that have total control over their thoughts, surely we can use this same power not only for our benefit, but also for the benefit of those around us. This will be reflected in our service and our compassion for others.

Maybe one day
We can turn and face our fears
Maybe one day
We can reach out through tears
After all it's really not that far
To where love can be found
Maybe one day
We can turn this world around

"Turn This World Around"
lyrics by Thomas, Grant, and Darnall
(Amy Grant)

SELECTED BIBLIOGRAPHY

Abraham, Jay. *Money-Making Secrets of Marketing Genius Jay Abraham.* Rolling Hills Estates, California: Abraham Publishing Group, Inc., 1993.

Allen, James. *As A Man Thinketh.* New York: Putnam Publishing Group, 1959.

Andrews, Andy. *Storms of Perfection: In Their Own Words.* Nashville, Tennessee: Lightning Crown Publishers, 1991.

Blechman, Bruce and Jay Conrad Levinson. *Guerrilla Financing: Alternative Techniques to Finance Any Small Business.* Boston: Houghton Mifflin Company, 1991.

Brown, Les. *The Power of Purpose: How to Create the Life You Always Wanted.* Niles, Illinois: Nightingale-Conant Corporation, 1998.

Covey, Stephen R. *First Things First: To Life, to Love, to Learn, to Leave a Legacy.* New York: Simon & Schuster, 1994.

_____. *The Seven Habits of Highly Effective People: Restoring the Character Ethic.* New York: Simon & Schuster, 1989.

Dell, Michael. *Direct from Dell: Strategies That Revolutionized an Industry.* New York: HarperCollins, 1999.

Dent, Harvey S., Jr. *The Roaring 2000s: Building the Wealth and Life Style You Desire in the Greatest Boom in History.* New York: Simon & Schuster, 1998.

Drucker, Peter F. *The Effective Executive.* New York: HarperBusiness, 1993.

Dyer, Wayne W. *You'll See It When You Believe It: The Way to Your Personal Transformation.* New York: Avon Books, 1989.

_____. *Your Erroneous Zones.* New York: HarperPaperbacks, 1993.

_____. *Your Sacred Self: Making the Decision to be Free.* New York: HarperPaperbacks, 1995.

Fuller, R. Buckminster. *Intuition.* New York: Anchor Books, 1973.

Greene, Bob and Oprah Winfrey. *Make the Connection: Ten Steps to a Better Body—and a Better Life.* New York: Hyperion, 1996.

Hill, Napoleon. *Think and Grow Rich.* Niles, Illinois: Nightingale-Conant Corporation, 1993.

Iacocca, Lee. *Iacocca: An Autobiography.* New York: Bantam Books, 1984.

Kersey, Cynthia. *Unstoppable: 45 Powerful Stories of Perseverance and Triumph from People Just Like You.* Naperville, Illinois: Sourcebooks, Inc., 1998.

Mackay, Harvey. *How to Build a Network of Power Relationships.* Niles, Illinois: Nightingale-Conant, 1995.

_____. *Pushing the Envelope: All the Way to the Top.* New York: Ballantine, 1999.

_____. *Swim with the Sharks Without Being Eaten Alive.* New York: William Morrow and Company, Inc., 1988.

Mandino, Og. *The Greatest Salesman in the World.* New York: Bantam, 1968.

McCormack, Mark. *What They Don't Teach You at Harvard Business School.* New York: Bantam Doubleday Dell Publishers, 1988.

Moore, Gary D. *Ten Golden Rules for Financial Success.* Grand Rapids, Michigan: Zondervan Publishing House, 1996.

Nightingale, Earl. *On Success.* Niles, Illinois: Nightingale-Conant Corporation, 1988.

Peale, Norman Vincent. *The Power of Positive Thinking.* Peale Foundation, Inc., 1995.

Pilzer, Paul Zane. *Unlimited Wealth: The Theory and Practice of Economic Alchemy.* New York: Crown Publishers, Inc., 1990.

Ries, Al. *Focus: The Future of Your Company Depends on It.* New York: HarperCollins, 1996.

Ries, Al and Jack Trout. *Positioning: The Battle for Your Mind.* New York: Warner Books, 1981.

_____. *The 22 Immutable Laws of Marketing.* New York: HarperBusiness, 1993.

Robbins, Anthony. *Awaken the Giant Within: How to Take Immediate Control of Your Mental, Emotional, Physical and Financial Destiny.* New York: Simon & Schuster, 1991.

_____. *Lessons in Mastery.* Niles, Illinois: Nightingale-Conant Corporation, 1998.

_____. *Living Health.* Niles, Illinois: Nightingale-Conant Corporation, 1991.

_____. *Personal Power II: The Driving Force.* San Diego: Robbins Research International, Inc., 1996.

_____. *PowerTalk Audio Magazine: Strategies for Lifelong Success.* San Diego: Robbins Research International, Inc., 1993.

_____. *Unlimited Power.* New York: Fawcett Columbine, 1986.

_____. *Unlimited Power: Home Study Course.* San Diego: Robbins Research International, Inc., 1991.

Schor, Juliet B. *The Overspent American: Upscaling, Downshifting, and the New Consumer.* New York: Basic Books, 1998.

Stanley, Thomas J. and William D. Danko. *The Millionaire Next Door: The Surprising Secrets of America's Wealthy.* Atlanta: Longstreet Press, Inc., 1996.

Templeton, John Marks. *Laws of Inner Wealth: Principles for Spiritual and Material Abundance.* Niles, Illinois: Nightingale-Conant Corporation, 1997.

_____. *Worldwide Laws of Life: 200 Eternal Spiritual Principles.* Philadelphia: Templeton Foundation Press, 1997.

Tracy, Brian. *How to Master Your Time: The Special Art of Increasing Your Productivity.* Niles, Illinois: Nightingale-Conant Corporation, 1989.

_____. *Maximum Achievement: Strategies and Skills That Will Unlock Your Hidden Powers to Succeed.* New York: Fireside, 1993.

_____. *The Luck Factor: How to Take the Chance Out of Becoming a Success.* Niles, Illinois: Nightingale-Conant Corporation, 1997.

_____. *Thinking Big: The Keys to Personal Power and Maximum Performance.* Niles, Illinois: Nightingale-Conant Corporation, 1996.

Walton, Sam. *Made in America: My Story.* New York: Doubleday, 1992.

Ziglar, Zig. *Top Performance: How to Develop Excellence in Yourself and Others.* Niles, Illinois: Nightingale-Conant Corporation, 1989.

For information about Dark Horse Recording or
about Robin Crow performances, contact:
Dark Horse Recording
2465 Old Charlotte Pike
Franklin, Tennessee 37064
or visit Robin's website at: www.robincrow.com
or www.darkhorserecording.com